THE MAGIC HOUR

100 Poems
from the Tuesday
Afternoon Poetry
Club

CHARLOTTE MOORE

Published in 2020 by Short Books,
an imprint of Octopus Publishing Group Ltd

Carmelite House
50 Victoria Embankment
London, EC4Y 0DZ
www.octopusbooks.co.uk

An Hachette UK Company
www.hachette.co.uk

10 9 8 7 6 5 4 3 2

A CIP catalogue record for this book is
available from the British Library.

ISBN: 978-1-78072-4263

Cover design by Micaela Alcaino
Interior illustrations by Annalise Orban

Printed and bound in Great Britain by
Clays Ltd, Elcograf S.p.A.

THE
MAGIC
HOUR

To everyone who has come to my house
on Tuesdays

Contents

3. Colour   69

4. Lovers, Courtship & Seduction   91

11. HEARTH & HOME

12. LOSS, AGE & DEATH

Introduction

> I give you the end of a golden string;
> Only wind it into a ball,
> It will lead you in at Heaven's gate,
> Built in Jerusalem's wall.
> *from "Jerusalem", William Blake*

A poem, said Robert Frost, "begins as a lump in the throat". He was talking about the creation of poetry, but something similar could be said about the experience of reading it. "Getting" a poem is a physical response. The scalp tingles, eyes prickle, stomach tightens. This response has not, at first, much to do with conscious thought. That comes later. Frost again: a poem is "a homesickness, a lovesickness. It is never a thought to begin with... It finds its thought or makes its thought."

People shy away from poetry because they think they won't understand it. They are put off older poems by an apparently uncrackable code of special vocabulary and classical or biblical allusions, while "modern" verse, with its abandonment of traditional form, seems wilfully hard to follow. How can the high walls be scaled, so that the reader can revel in the glory and interest that lie on the other side – the "imaginary gardens, with real toads in them", in Marianne Moore's words? Sensing that many people want to explore the possibilities of poetry but are unsure how to go about it, in the summer of 2018 I started a weekly reading group on Tuesday afternoons at my home in Sussex.

English, its huge vocabulary fed through the centuries by the languages and dialects of the conquerors and the conquered, is a fertile seedbed. Our poetic heritage is unrivalled; we are more literary than we realise. When we say that ours is not to reason why or express the opinion that it's better to have loved and lost than never to have loved at all, we may not know that we're channelling Tennyson, or that Shakespeare gave our journalists their sea changes and winters of discontent, or that we owe our season of mists and mellow fruitfulness to Keats, but such phrases and hundreds like them are used every day. And most people, even those who deny all patience with poetry, have their own store of the stuff, in the form of song lyrics, nursery rhymes, hymns, carols, even advertising and media soundbites. "As a very small child I was made to sing carols to my grumpy Grandad, which were stories in themselves," said Veronica, a member of the group; "also many hymns of which I am really fond to this day." Words click together; a phrase becomes more than the sum of its parts. There is resonance that transcends logical meaning. The words delight us, excite us, console us, remind us of moments of personal significance. This is the foundation for real love and knowledge, a knowledge that becomes a source of lifelong pleasure and nourishment. "My father, a welder with a tough life, would rhyme many words," recalls Veronica. "Language was enjoyed. Remember, Remember, the Fifth of November... Would you like a story about Jackanory? Shall I begin it? That's all there is in it... Children get continually sucked into rhyme."

The Tuesday afternoon sessions were sparked by my giving some A level tuition on Keats, after many years away from teaching; sitting at home in an armchair talking about "Ode to a Nightingale" struck me as an immensely pleasurable and stimulating thing to do, but how good it would be to escape the constraints of the academic syllabus and talk about poems in whichever way took my fancy... So I sent out a flyer, and a group of people started arriving for coffee and biscuits and two hours of poetic immersion. Some came with lots of literary background, some with little or none. Either is fine; the mixture is fruitful. Some come every week, others drop in occasionally. Again, that's a good thing. Changes prevent staleness, and it's always interesting to see who'll turn up.

My aim is to take the fear out of poetry; the fear that

it will make you feel stupid, and the fear that you'll be bored. Such fears have their roots in schooldays. Some members of the group recalled having to learn poems as a punishment, others had felt humiliated by the mockery of teachers. "I've always thought that in a few phrases poetry can say so very much," said Veronica, "but I suffered from Mrs Evans. Perhaps I asked too many questions." David, a schoolboy in the progressive 1960s, had been taught that poems which rhymed and scanned were intrinsically inferior to experimental "free verse"; his own strong response to rhythm and musicality had led him to suspect that precious babies had been thrown out with much stale bathwater. Others felt they simply hadn't been introduced to poetry at all. Caroline T, who took A levels in maths, physics and chemistry, always felt deprived. "A series of sonnets formed the basis of a general studies lesson, which I enjoyed," she remembered, "but it was a one-off experience and led nowhere. I was caught up in a great divide between science and the arts that took place in schools at that time and have always been saddened by losing that part of my education and, in a way, part of myself as well. It has been a great joy to rediscover poetry and my reactions to it. Of particular value to me is the way poetry bypasses my analytical 'left brain' way of being, triggering imaginative and emotional responses in valuable ways – ones that can easily be shut down in our culture that praises busyness and functionality over almost everything else."

Of course, there are plenty of positive school experiences. Polly, who arrived at our first session with poems fluttering out of her bag, fell under poetry's thrall when she was taught Robert Browning's "A Toccatta of Galuppi's" and Tennyson's "Maud"; she still treasures her textbooks with their teenage annotations, and can quote "reams of *Romeo and Juliet* by heart. As a teenager, poetry blew me away, and it's been the mainstay of my life ever since." Pam, a retired teacher of English who particularly loves Walter de la Mare, Charles Causley, George Herbert and Laurie Lee, used their poems as springboards for her pupils' creative writing, and remembers the results with affection half a century later. Sue recalled, "I once worked in a school where the head of English hated poetry: my job was to teach it to every class. I found the best initial approach was to stress the practical value of poems, on all occasions. What began as a bit of a joke has come curiously true. After four hours' difficult driving to visit a favourite brother-in-law who had an aggressive cancer, I came home shattered and very sad – BUT there was just enough time to get to your house for a session. And, as always, it worked."

I wanted the Tuesday sessions to be free of any sense that poems are rungs on a ladder leading to some kind of academic achievement. At the same time, I didn't want to dumb down. Ignorance isn't helpful, and most people enjoy finding out something about the context of a poem and the life story of the poet. It's more that reading poetry is its own reward. It refreshes the parts that other art forms cannot reach, or at any rate it reaches those parts through different channels.

Most weeks, I choose about eight poems touching on a similar theme, some well known, some less so. I mix poems which have an instant appeal or impact with relatively "difficult" ones which respond to slower scrutiny. I find them, mainly, by trawling through the many, many anthologies that lurk in blue-green Edwardian dimness on the shelves of my book-crammed house, a house which is the repository for the possessions of family members living and dead. The anthologies often contain letters, postcards, inscriptions, comments and doodles; layers of the archaeology of appreciation. Palgrave's *Golden Treasury*, *Other Men's Flowers*, *The Dragon Book of Verse*, *The Faber Book of Children's Verse* (pleasingly full of poems about crime and drunkenness), James Reeves' *The Poet's World*, Clifford Bax's *Vintage Verse*, *The Pageant of Poetry*, or, from mid-century, geometrically decorated volumes with obsolescence built into their titles such as *Poets of Our Time* or *7 Themes in Modern Verse*... These, and a great many more, are augmented by market-stall finds, or by suggestions from members of the group. I swallow poems by the gallon. I have no preconceptions about what I'm looking for; I just read on until something hits the spot. I read them aloud to the group, aiming for clarity rather than performance; I provide a little bit of context, and then find out what people think. "When you hand over the copies of the poem we are about to look at, I never read it, as I want to hear it for the first time when you read it out," says Sarah N, a singer with an acute ear. "When we read Christopher Smart's 'My Cat Jeoffrey' I went home and sang it in plainsong and discovered it to be utterly made to be thus sung."

Often, the poems shine a light into corners, and people start talking about all sorts of things. Reading Emily Brontë's "Remembrance", Judith said, "it says something so integral about the human condition post a certain age. The first time I recognised it was in the shape of my poor Mum just after her utterly beloved husband had died. Literally her shape had been changed by the sorrow and then gradually she rallied just as in the poem."

"It's gentle balm for the soul," said Sue. "Really, the essence of these Tuesdays is the sheer delight of continuing to learn about poetry, about each other, about life. I always come away thoroughly invigorated and encouraged to soldier on." For Pam, who is blind, but who carries a great many poems in her memory, the group has been "a resurrection".

This book is a collection of some of the poems we've read. It's not meant to be a potted guide to English verse. I'm very much aware that I've left out many great poets, including some of my own favourites. I'm also aware that it barely touches on what's being written now, in the first quarter of the 21st century. (Blame the copyright expenses of using work by living poets for this, as well as my habit of burrowing through my beloved faded anthologies). I've presented the poems here in the version in which I found them; my own preference is to use original spelling wherever possible but I haven't always managed to track it down. I've allowed only one poem per poet, with the exception of several by everybody's favourite, Anon.

Poetry, said John Berryman, adds to the stock of available reality. I hope this book will help to do exactly that.

Charlotte Moore, 27 April 2020

1

EARTH, AIR, FIRE
& WATER

For centuries, people believed that all matter was based on a combination of the four elements – earth, air, fire and water. For poets, the elements are a short-cut to the complexities of thoughts and emotions as well as physical substance. Robert Frost's masculine identity is rooted in earth; Carol Ann Duffy's passion is sanctified by water; Robert Southwell's transcendent vision is expressed in fire, while W.B. Yeats miraculously combines all the elements in his attempt to remake himself. Any number of poems could have been included in this section; the elements are at the core of everything.

To Earthward

BY ROBERT FROST 1874–1963

Love at the lips was touch
As sweet as I could bear;
And once that seemed too much
I lived on air

That crossed me from sweet things,
The flow of – was it musk
From hidden grapevine springs
Down hill at dusk?

I had the swirl and ache
From sprays of honeysuckle
That when they're gathered shake
Dew on the knuckle.

I craved strong sweets, but those
Seemed strong when I was young:
The petal of the rose
It was that stung.

Now no joy but lacks salt
That is not dashed with pain
And weariness and fault;
I crave the stain

Of tears, the aftermark
Of almost too much love,
The sweet of bitter bark
And burning clove.

When stiff and sore and scarred
I take away my hand
From leaning on it hard
In grass and sand,

The hurt is not enough:
I long for weight and strength
To feel the earth as rough
To all my length.

Polly, a founder member of the Tuesday group, stumbled upon Frost when she was 16, through Simon & Garfunkel's "The Dangling Conversation" – "And you read your Emily Dickinson and I my Robert Frost, and we note our place with bookmarks that measure what we've lost." As Polly put it, "Gosh, what a discovery! Two of my favourite poets in one hit! It led to a lifelong passion for both poets. Poems like 'To Earthward' mean so much to me, they've been part of my life for so long I almost feel as if I wrote them. When I was young, 'To

Earthward' immediately touched my heart. It felt like a love poem written to Nature and yet pierced with the knowledge that one day such tender love alone will not be enough but will need to be somehow felt more deeply. Now I'm old it still moves me. There are still joys that are not yet 'dashed with pain and weariness and fault', but I know exactly what he means."

The Night is Darkening Round Me

BY EMILY BRONTË 1818–1848

The night is darkening round me,
The wild winds coldly blow;
But a tyrant spell has bound me,
And I cannot, cannot go.

The giant trees are bending
Their bare boughs weighed with snow;
The storm is fast descending,
And yet I cannot go.

Clouds beyond clouds above me,
Wastes beyond wastes below;
But nothing drear can move me;
I will not, cannot go.

Several members of the group, myself included, were smitten with the Brontë family at an early age. The speaker in this poem is a character from the fantasy worlds – Glass Town, Angria and Gondal – created and shared by the Brontë siblings in their windswept, isolated childhoods, and developed in adult life.

"She gives you a sense of tremendous oppression and tremendous possibility, both at the same time," said Shelagh.

The Burning Babe

BY ST ROBERT SOUTHWELL C.1561–1595

As I in hoary winter's night stood shivering in the snow,
Surprised I was with sudden heat which made my heart
   to glow;
And lifting up a fearful eye to view what fire was near,
A pretty Babe all burning bright did in the air appear;
Who, scorched with excessive heat, such floods of tears
   did shed
As though his floods should quench his flames which
   with his tears were fed.
"Alas!" quoth he, "but newly born, in fiery heats I fry,
Yet none approach to warm their hearts or feel my fire
   but I.
My faultless breast the furnace is, the fuel wounding
   thorns,
Love is the fire, and sighs the smoke, the ashes shames
   and scorns;
The fuel Justice layeth on, and Mercy blows the coals,
The metal in this furnace wrought are men's defiled souls,
For which, as now on fire I am to work them to their
   good,
So will I melt into a bath, to wash them in my blood."
With this he vanished out of sight, and swiftly shrunk
   away
And straight I called unto mind that it was Christmas
   day.

A shining, passionate poem about Christian redemption. Robert Southwell was a young Jesuit priest who fell foul of Elizabeth I's recusancy laws. After six years of clandestinely celebrating Mass he was hunted, captured and tortured by Elizabeth's "pursuivant" Richard Topcliffe. He wrote "The Burning Babe" while in solitary confinement in the Tower of London.

Southwell was a distant cousin of William Shakespeare. He dedicated his posthumously published collection of poems, *St Peter's Complaint*, "to my worthy good cosen Maister W.S." Was he hoping to convert him?

On 21 February 1595 Southwell was hanged, drawn and quartered, not long before Shakespeare delighted the Queen with *A Midsummer Night's Dream*, apparently unmoved by his cousin's fate. But perhaps the striking imagery of "The Burning Babe" did creep into Shakespeare's mind, as when a decade later Macbeth envisages "Pity, like a naked newborn babe,/Striding the blast."

The "fiery heats" in which the poor Babe fries parallel the purgatorial fires of Roman Catholicism, in which souls are purged of sin to ready them for Heaven. Southwell uses the apparatus of chemistry, perhaps of alchemy, to describe how our "defiled souls" can be purified and remade through Christ's suffering love – the furnace, the fuel, the heating of the metal and the chemical bath. But this transformative process must involve pain and effort on our part. Southwell was prepared to die for his faith, confident in the promise of redemption. His poem calls us to recognise that a true understanding of the Christmas gift of salvation must incorporate a foreshadowing of the "thorns" of the Crucifixion.

Southwell was canonised in 1970, the only bona fide saint represented in this anthology.

Witch Burning

BY SYLVIA PLATH, 1932–1963
from POEM FOR A BIRTHDAY

In the marketplace they are piling the dry sticks.
A thicket of shadows is a poor coat. I inhabit
The wax image of myself, a doll's body.
Sickness begins here: I am the dartboard for witches.
Only the devil can eat the devil out.
In the month of red leaves I climb onto a bed of fire.

It is easy to blame the dark; the mouth of a door,
The cellar's belly. They've blown my sparkler out.
A black-sharded lady keeps me in a parrot cage.
What large eyes the dead have!
I am intimate with a hairy spirit.
Smoke wheels from the beak of this empty jar.

If I am a little one, I can do no harm.
If I don't move about, I'll knock nothing over. So I said,
Sitting under a potlid, tiny and inert as a rice grain.
They are turning the burners up, ring after ring.
We are full of starch, my small white fellows. We grow.
It hurts at first. The red tongues will teach the truth.

Mother of beetles, only unclench your hand:
I'll fly through the candle's mouth like a singeless moth.
Give me back my shape. I am ready to construe the days
I coupled with dust in the shadow of a stone.
My ankles brighten. Brightness ascends my thighs.
I am lost, I am lost, in the robes of all this light.

"When we read this," Sarah N commented, looking around the group, "we women all understood her state of mind but the men were somewhat bewildered, bordering on alienated." Those women who were mothers of troubled daughters or had vivid memories of their tormented younger selves fell upon it with cries of recognition. Plath, a New Englander, draws much of her imagery from the 17th-century Salem witch trials and knits it together with confining domesticity (the rice cooking) and her own experience of electric shock treatment for mental "illness". Also, as an Englishwoman by adoption, she would have been in bonfire mood in early November, when she wrote it.

The horror is transcended by the ending. "There's something triumphant about that last line," Judith said.

On Westwall Downes

BY WILLIAM STRODE C.1602–1645

When Westwall Downes I gan to tread,
Where cleanely wynds the greene did sweepe,
Methought a landskipp there was spread,
Here a bush and there a sheepe:
The pleated wrinkles of the face
Of wave-swolne earth did lend such grace,
As shadowings in Imag'ry
Which both deceive and please the eye.

The sheepe sometymes did tread the maze
By often wynding in and in,
And sometymes round about they trace
Which mylkmayds call a Fairie ring:
Such semicircles have they runne,
Such lines across so trimly spunne
That sheppeards learne whenere they please
A new Geometry with ease.

The slender food upon the downe
Is allwayes even, allwayes bare,
Which neither spring nor winter's frowne
Can ought improve or ought impayre:
Such is the barren Eunuches chynne,

Which thus doth evermore begynne
With tender downe to be orecast
Which never comes to haire at last.

Here and there twoe hilly crests
Amiddst them hugg a pleasant greene,
And these are like twoe swelling breasts
That close a tendre fall betweene.
Here would I sleepe, or read, or pray
From early morn till flight of day:
But harke! a sheepe-bell calls mee upp,
Like Oxford colledge-bells, to supp.

The cheery Cavalier poet William Strode was Public Orator at Oxford; as the last line suggests, his life was pleasantly regulated by "colledge-bells". I do like the flavour of the original spelling, so I've left it, but it helps if you read "ought" as "aught" ("anything/in any way"), and "orecast" is "overcast".

"The way he makes comparisons between the landscape and human life is delightful," said Sarah N. Amanda was cheered by the fact that he sees wrinkles as "lending grace" to a face. "I identify with the sense it gives of the landscape being laid out to enter into and join with," said Caroline T, "and the swelling breasts somehow manage to be surprisingly sensual and appropriate as well as cringingly embarrassing."

"Landskipp", a Dutch painters' term, was first recorded in England in 1598, so Strode's use of it is quite up to date. A "landskipp" suggests nature arranged or organised for Man's delight and instruction.

To Winter

BY WILLIAM BLAKE 1757–1827

O Winter! bar thine adamantine doors:
The north is thine: there hast thou built thy dark
Deep-founded habitation. Shake not thy roofs
Nor bend thy pillars with thine iron car.

He hears me not, but o'er the yawning deep
Rides heavy; his storms are unchain'd, sheathed
In ribbed steel; I dare not lift mine eyes;
For he hath rear'd his sceptre o'er the world.

Lo! now the direful monster, whose skin clings
To his strong bones, strides o'er the groaning rocks:
He withers all in silence, and in his hand
Unclothes the earth, and freezes up frail life.

He takes his seat upon the cliffs, the mariner
Cries in vain. Poor little wretch! that deal'st
With storms; till heaven smiles, and the monster
Is driven yelling to his caves beneath Mount Hecla.

Old Testament meets Milton meets Industrial Revolution, with startlingly original effect. The commands of the first verse seem powerful enough to keep an enemy at bay, so it's a shock to find in the second verse that the anti-god Winter swats them away unheeded. In a reversal of the opening chapter of Genesis, Winter's hand "unclothes the earth". Mankind cowers as his iron chariot careers across the world; the brave sailor becomes as pitiful as a naked infant – a favourite image for Blake in his later poetry. But though we can't see how Winter's reign can be broken, God can. One smile from Heaven, and it's Spring. Winter shrinks – still a fearsome monster, but one that can be chased into a cave, and confined, at least for the time being.

Mount Hecla is a volcano in Iceland, named the gateway to Hell after a tremendous eruption in 1104. Witches were believed to gather there at Easter (another scriptural inversion?) and the birds flying round it were damned souls.

"It's marvellous that he doesn't use rhyme," said Michael W. It's a short poem but it feels massive, awe-inspiring. The iambic pentameter, the flexible five-stress line, is used throughout, its regularity disrupted by hefty mid-line punctuation. Blake wrote this when he was still in his teens. The image of "the direful monster, whose skin clings/To his strong bones" striding over the "groaning rocks" made us think of Frankenstein's monster. Mary Shelley, another teenage writer, created him 40 years later, and had him hurtling and howling over icy Arctic scenery; incidentally, she wrote her novel when the eruption of a different volcano had cast a winter chill over a European summer. It feels as if she knew this poem; as Blake, an artist as well as a poet, had provided illustrations for her mother Mary Wollstonecraft's *Original Stories* for children, it's quite possible that she did.

Miranda Seymour, Mary Shelley's biographer, writes that one of these illustrations "showed two dead children lying under the gaze of a tall, gaunt man, not quite human. Someone must have read Mary the accompanying story, of how the man ran away from civilisation to live alone, dependent on the kindness of passing strangers. Was it here that the idea of *Frankenstein* was born?"

River

BY CAROL ANN DUFFY 1955–

Down by the river, under the trees, love waits for me
to walk from the journeying years of my time and arrive.
I part the leaves and they toss me a blessing of rain.

The river stirs and turns, consoling and fondling itself
with watery hands, its clear limbs parting and closing.
Grey as a secret, the heron bows its head on the bank.

I drop my past on the grass and open my arms, which ache
as though they held up this heavy sky, or had pressed
against window glass all night as my eyes sieved the stars;

open my mouth, wordless at last meeting love at last, dry
from travelling so long, shy of a prayer. You step from
   the shade,
and I feel love come to my arms and cover my mouth, feel

my soul swoop and ease itself into my skin, like a bird
threading a river. Then I can look love full in the face, see
who you are I have come this far to find, the love of my life.

"River" is one of a series of 51 poems describing the course of a love affair, from its nervy beginning to its passionate apex to its perhaps inevitable end. The sequence, published as *Rapture*, consciously belongs to an English lyric tradition, one that includes Elizabethan poets such as Spenser and Shakespeare as well as the Victorian Elizabeth Barrett Browning's *Sonnets from the Portuguese* and lesser-known sequences such as the "Juliet" poems of Wilfrid Scawen Blunt (see page 73). Like her forebears, Carol Ann Duffy mixes the public and the personal to memorable effect.

In "River", the affair has reached its peak of purity and intensity. Water – the river and the rain – blesses the lovers as if in a marriage service combined with a baptism. Time almost stands still; briefly, past and future can be forgotten: "I drop my past on the grass," like a discarded garment. The poem celebrates a moment of arrival. But such a moment cannot last for ever; the river and Time must both move on. Perhaps this is the grey secret the watching heron knows.

"I was really surprised how this one hit me in the stomach when you read it aloud," said Cresta, recalling an early meeting of the group. "Some poems have such a strong afterlife. I haven't read that one since, but now, six months later, it is still in my mind."

Sailing to Byzantium

BY W.B. YEATS 1865–1939

That is no country for old men. The young
In one another's arms, birds in the trees,
– Those dying generations – at their song,
The salmon-falls, the mackerel-crowded seas,
Fish, flesh or fowl, commend all summer long
Whatever is begotten, born, and dies.
Caught in that sensual music all neglect
Monuments of unageing intellect.

An aged man is but a paltry thing,
A tattered coat upon a stick, unless
Soul clap its hands and sing, and louder sing
For every tatter in its mortal dress,
Nor is there singing school but studying
Monuments of its own magnificence;
And therefore I have sailed the seas and come
To the holy city of Byzantium.

O sages standing in God's holy fire
As in the gold mosaic of a wall,
Come from the holy fire, perne in a gyre,
And be the singing-masters of my soul.
Consume my heart away; sick with desire
And fastened to a dying animal
It knows not what it is; and gather me
Into the artifice of eternity.

Once out of nature I shall never take
My bodily form from any natural thing,
But such a form as Grecian goldsmiths make
Of hammered gold and gold enamelling
To keep a drowsy Emperor awake;
Or set upon a golden bough to sing
To lords and ladies of Byzantium
Of what is past, or passing, or to come.

Sixty-year-old Yeats goes on a spiritual journey. His body is "a dying animal"; his heart, still "sick with desire", is no use to him in Ireland, the country of the sexually and emotionally active young. All that is left to him is his soul, and it is his responsibility as a poet to make his soul sing. Metaphorically, he sails to Byzantium, to achieve some kind of artistic permanence.

Why Byzantium? Yeats explained: "When Irishmen were illuminating the *Book of Kells*, and making the jewelled croziers in the [Dublin] National Museum, Byzantium was the centre of European civilisation and the source of its spiritual philosophy, so I symbolise the search for the spiritual life by a journey to that city." For Elizabeth, who particularly loves this poem, it "reminded me of the awe and love I felt for Salisbury Cathedral, where I grew up. This was the monument of my earliest memories."

What on earth does "perne in a gyre" mean? Yeats had a somewhat arcane set of beliefs about history and spirituality moving in cycles. Don't let this become a stumbling block. When I read these lines, I see the sages stepping out of the holy fire and spinning like whirling dervishes. Their spinning is the mystic ritual needed to liberate Yeats from his ageing mortal self and draw him into "the artifice of eternity". I don't know whether Yeats imagined this, but it works for me. This isn't an easy poem, but Yeats' lyrical gift is so powerful that when I first read it, at school aged 16 and hardly understanding a line of it, the words seemed to swim or sail off the page.

"Exact meaning is elusive and mysterious," said Elizabeth, "but it doesn't matter, it's all lovely. And the central message of the second verse – 'soul clap its hands and sing' – is clear as a bell. I think of my mother's sad hatred and fear of old age and her suicidal wishes; there seemed to be no hope of encouraging her to love life while it lasted. She was obsessed with her tattered coat upon a stick."

In the last verse, Yeats seems dismissive of the artistic permanence he has achieved. Yes, he's a beautiful mechanical bird, made of gold and on a golden bough; he's escaped from the "dying animal" condition. But he's small and trivial, and no one's really listening to his songs. However, he was wrong about this. Nearly a century later, here you are reading this truly great poem about mind, body, heart and soul; you've sailed with him to Byzantium.

2

PARENT & CHILD

Tragic poems about parents and children are more plentiful than happy ones, perhaps because a parent and child in harmony presents such a perfect whole that there is no space for a poem to grow. In traditional songs and nursery rhymes, parents are, on the whole, a punitive, oppressive breed – such songs are a way of expressing rebellion or subversion, as seen here in "My Mother Said I Never Should".

Henry I to the Sea (1120 AD)

BY EUGENE LEE-HAMILTON 1845–1907

O Sea, take all, since thou hast taken him
Whose life to me was life. Let one wide wave
Now sweep this land, and make a single grave
For king and people. Let the wild gull skim

Where now is England, and the sea-fish swim
In every drowned cathedral's vaulted nave,
As in a green and pillared ocean cave,
Submerged for ever and for ever dim.

And if the shuddering pilot ventures there
And sees their pinnacles, like rocks to shun,
Above the waves, and green with tidal hair,

Then let him whisper that this thing was done
By God, the Lord of Oceans, at the prayer
Of England's king, who mourned his only son.

What a feat of imagination this is. The speaker is Henry
I, king of England, who has learned that his beloved son

and only male heir has been drowned in the wreck of the White Ship, in the Channel off the Normandy coast; he must find expression for his illimitable grief. If his son has gone, then England must go too; the great cathedrals, marvels of the age, must lie submerged, like drowned bodies ("with tidal hair"), their pinnacles as dangerous as the rocks on which the White Ship foundered. Political and spiritual power, even life itself, have no meaning now that the prince, the son, is dead.

The destructive immensity of feeling, the arrogance justified by the depth of love and loss, recall *King Lear.* "It's actually really beautiful," said Sue in surprise; she had been expecting something more heavily historical, the poetic equivalent of an over-carved Victorian sideboard. Metaphorically at least, the death of the heir did (almost) submerge England. After Henry's death, his daughter Matilda and her cousin Stephen thrashed it out in a bitter and ruinous civil war – a contemporary chronicler described it as "nineteen long winters when Christ and his saints slept".

Eugene Lee-Hamilton, aesthete and diplomat, suddenly lost the use of his legs during his twenties. He remained bedbound and in pain for many years, unable even to hold a pen; he dictated his poems, many of which contain images of being buried, drowned or held captive. He eventually experienced a miracle cure and re-entered life "with the zest of an undergraduate".

The Magic Hour

Australian Bill

BY W.H. DAVIES 1871–1940

Australian Bill is dying fast,
For he's a drunken fool:
He either sits in an alehouse,
Or stands outside a school.

He left this house of ours at seven,
And he was drunk by nine;
And when I passed him near a school
He nods his head to mine.

When Bill took to the hospital,
Sick, money he had none –
He came forth well, but lo! his home,
His wife and child had gone.

"I'll watch a strange school every day,
Until the child I see;
For Liz will send the child to school –
No doubt of that", says he.

And "Balmy" Tom is near as bad,
A-drinking ale till blind:
No absent child grieves he, but there's
A dead love on his mind.
But Bill, poor Bill, is dying fast,

For he's the greater fool;
He either sits in an alehouse
Or stands outside a school.

William Henry Davies was a juvenile delinquent from Newport who ran away to sea. He tramped through America, sometimes working, sometimes begging, until he lost a leg jumping onto a freight train to get a free ride. Back in Britain, he slept rough or in dosshouses, composing his poems in secret. "Australian Bill" describes one of his dosshouse companions. Davies tells the story of Bill's downfall in unadorned language. This wreck of a man never gives up on the precious and pathetic hope that he will see his child again. In the hands of a Victorian moralist, Bill's faith would be rewarded (and liquor would be eschewed), but Davies is a realist. Bill is "the greater fool" for clinging on to the forlorn hope. Davies is bitter and uncompromising about the fate of Bill, Balmy Tom, and, by implication, himself, but that single word "poor" in the final verse reveals a sympathy all the more poignant for its restraint.

"I like poems that tell a story," said Mike F, "and when you find out some background of the author and the poem, that makes it part of a larger story."

Elsa Wertman

BY EDGAR LEE MASTERS 1868–1950

I was a peasant girl from Germany,
Blue-eyed, rosy, happy and strong.
And the first place I worked was at Thomas Greene's.
On a summer's day when she was away
He stole into the kitchen and took me
Right in his arms and kissed me on my throat,
I turning my head. Then neither of us seemed to know
 what happened.
And I cried for what would become of me.
And cried and cried as my secret began to show.
One day Mrs. Greene said she understood,
And would make no trouble for me,
And, being childless, would adopt it.
(He had given her a farm to be still.)
So she hid in the house and sent out rumors,
As if it were going to happen to her.
And all went well and the child was born – they were so
 kind to me.
Later I married Gus Wertman, and years passed.
But – at political rallies when sitters-by thought I was
 crying
At the eloquence of Hamilton Greene –
That was not it.
No! I wanted to say:
That's my son! That's my son!

"It's a whole novel condensed into a few lines," said Pepe. "'They were so kind to me' – ooh, that's painful," said Judith. David was struck by the modernity of the tone, and the way Elsa tells her own story in her own language, with no authorial intervention.

Edgar Lee Masters was a lawyer as well as a poet and dramatist, and earned a reputation as a defender of the poor. "Elsa Wertman" is one of the free verse "epitaphs" in his *Spoon River Anthology*, set in a fictionalised small town in Masters' home state of Illinois. "It's a rare man who understands what it feels like to give up a child," said Cresta. "The poem has a gentle rhythm, and what appears to be quiet and delicate reveals a fierce anger on behalf of the exploited girl who weeps for the loss of her son. It's politics by stealth, poetry to change the way you think."

Yorkshire Wife's Saga

BY RUTH PITTER 1897–1992

War was her life, with want and the wild air;
Not for life only; she was out to win.
Houses and ground were cheap, out on the bare
Moor, and the land not bad; they could begin,
Now that the seven sons were mostly men.

Two acres and a sow, on hard-saved brass;
Men down the mine, and mother did the rest.
Pity, with all those sons, they had no lass;
No help, no talk, no mutual interest,
Made fourteen slaving hours empty at best.

Fierce winter mornings, up at three or four;
Men bawl, pigs shriek against the raving beck.
Off go the eight across the mile of moor,
With well-filled dinner-pail and sweat-ragged neck;
But pigs still shriek, and wind blows door off sneck.

Of course they made it; what on earth could stop
People like that? Marrying one by one,
This got a farm, the other got a shop;
Now she was left with but the youngest son,
But she could look about and feel she'd won.

Doctor had told her she was clean worn out.
All pulled to bits, and nowt that he could do.
But plenty get that way, or die, without
Having a ruddy ten-quid note to show.
She'd got seven thriving sons all in a row.

And grandchildren. She liked going by bus
Or train, to stay a bit in those snug homes.
They were her colonies, fair glorious.
"Sit by the fire, ma, till the dinner comes.
Sit by the fire and cuddle little lass."

"It's interesting", said Sue, "that her story is told in tradi-
tionally male language." Winning wars, building empires,
colonising... the "saga" of the title puts the Yorkshire
Wife on a level with the heroes of ancient times. "This is
the story of the 20th century," said Michael W, "from the
elemental bare moor and 'raving beck' to the buses and
trains and the snug homes...".

The complete absence of sentimentality in the bulk
of the poem – shrieking pigs and uncommunicative men
– makes the concluding reward of the little granddaughter particularly touching.

A sneck is a latch.

My Mother Said I Never Should

ANON. UNDATEABLE

My mother said I never should
Play with the gypsies in the wood
If I did she would say
Naughty girl to disobey!
Your hair shan't curl, your shoes shan't shine
You gypsy girl, you shan't be mine!
My father said that if I did
He'd rap my head with a teapot lid.
The wood was dark, the grass was green,
In came Sally with a tambourine.
I went to the sea, no ship to get across,
I paid six shillings for a blind white horse.
I up on his back and was off in a crack –
Sally tell my mother I shall never come back.

This had all the women in the group chanting in play-ground rhythm – "Oh, I remember this! It's a skipping rhyme," said Pepe. It is indeed, and one of which the origins remain obscure. As with all rhymes well handled by generations of children, there are many variants. The version given here is the one that stuck in my mind.

It's one of the most atmospheric poems I know. "The wood was dark, the grass was green,/ In came Sally with a tambourine" – what could be more enticing than that? The threats of the parents are feeble in comparison; what do they and their world have to offer?

The Toys

BY COVENTRY PATMORE 1823–1896

My little Son, who look'd from thoughtful eyes
And moved and spoke in quiet grown-up wise,
Having my law the seventh time disobey'd,
I struck him, and dismiss'd
With hard words and unkiss'd,
His Mother, who was patient, being dead.
Then, fearing lest his grief should hinder sleep,
I visited his bed,
But found him slumbering deep,
With darken'd eyelids, and their lashes yet
From his late sobbing wet.
And I, with moan,
Kissing away his tears, left others of my own;
For, on a table drawn beside his head,
He had put, within his reach,
A box of counters and a red-vein'd stone,
A piece of glass abraded by the beach
And six or seven shells,
A bottle with bluebells
And two French copper coins, ranged there with
    careful art,
To comfort his sad heart.
So when that night I pray'd
To God, I wept, and said:

Ah, when at last we lie with tranced breath,
Not vexing Thee in death,
And Thou rememberest of what toys
We made our joys,
How weakly understood,
Thy great commanded good,
Then, fatherly not less
Than I whom Thou hast moulded from the clay,
Thou'lt leave Thy wrath, and say,
"I will be sorry for their childishness."

Coventry Patmore wrote his long narrative poem "The Angel in the House" about his first marriage. When his wife Emily died, leaving him with six young children, the themes of his poetry turned to grief and loss. "The Toys" draws a very Victorian moral parallel between the earthly and the heavenly father; Patmore prays that his Creator will show more understanding of his own "childishness" than he himself managed to show towards his son. But it also feels modern in its description of the lonely single parent's loss of patience, so soon followed by remorse. "'Unkiss'd' is such a sad word," said Pam, "and the wet eyelashes tug at your heart." The list of treasures led to a flood of reminiscences about the talismans that our own children had used to comfort their sad hearts.

Eden Rock

BY CHARLES CAUSLEY 1917–2003

They are waiting for me somewhere beyond Eden Rock:
My father, twenty-five, in the same suit
Of Genuine Irish Tweed, his terrier Jack
Still two years old and trembling at his feet.

My mother, twenty-three, in a sprigged dress
Drawn at the waist, ribbon in her straw hat,
Has spread the stiff, white cloth over the grass.
Her hair, the colour of wheat, takes on the light.

She pours tea from a Thermos, the milk straight
From an old H.P. sauce-bottle, a screw
Of paper for a cork; slowly sets out
The same three plates, the tin cups painted blue.

The sky whitens as if lit by three suns.
My mother shades her eyes and looks my way
Over the drifted stream. My father spins
A stone along the water. Leisurely,

They beckon to me from the other bank.
I hear them call, "See where the stream-path is!
Crossing is not as hard as you might think."

I had not thought that it would be like this.

This immediately accessible yet mysterious poem touched all of us. Several people recalled the death of their parents and a sense of the numinous, a feeling of being called or beckoned. "Not long before my mother died," said Amanda, "I sat through the night with her, because I thought the end was near. Suddenly she called out, 'I'm coming! I'm coming! Wait for me!' I held her hands and said, 'No, you're not going anywhere; stay with me.' She survived the night, and in the morning I asked if she remembered anything about it. 'Oh yes,' she said, 'I was standing on the bank of a wide river, and on the opposite side I could see all the dogs I've ever had, calling for me to cross over.' Dogs, mind you – not people!"

Causley anchors us with reality – the trembling terrier, the H.P. sauce-bottle – then almost imperceptibly draws us into a realm which is both known and not known. The first clue is his mother's hair taking on the light. Then there's the link between the three people, the three plates, all very much there, and the three suns, both there and not there. By the end of the poem, the rock, the stream and the bank are much, much more than just a suitable spot for a picnic, and "stream-path" becomes infinitely suggestive.

Causley was an only child, and a devoted one. His

father, a Cornish groom and gardener, died as a long-term result of Great War wounds when Charles was only seven; at 15, Charles had to leave school to earn enough to keep himself and his mother. He never married, and nursed his mother for the last six years of her life following a stroke.

Causley was often asked where Eden Rock is. "I made it up – Dartmoor, I said. That's always a safe answer."

A Melancholy Lay

BY MARJORIE FLEMING AGED 8, C.1811

Three Turkeys fair their last have breathed
And now this world for ever leaved
Their father and their mother too
Will sigh and weep as well as you
Mourning for their offspring fair
Whom they did nurse with tender care
Indeed the rats their bones have cranch'd
To Eternity they are launch'd
Their graceful form and pretty eyes
Their fellow fowls did not despise
A direful death indeed they had
That would put any parent mad
But she was more than usual calm
She did not give a single dam
Here ends this melancholy lay
Farewell poor turkeys I must say.

Not many poems have made us laugh aloud, but who could fail to chortle at Mrs Turkey's phlegmatic response to her bereavement? Those of us who are parents are familiar with elegies produced by our offspring of the "Here lies a faithful hamster" variety, and Marjorie Fleming shows herself mistress of the genre. "It's just a pity she didn't rhyme 'cranch'd' with 'lunched'," said Michael W.

We don't need to think of a well-brought-up eight-year-old girl uttering profanities; a dam was a small Indian copper coin, almost worthless. The expression "I don't give a dam" had entered the English language due to the ever-strengthening British presence in India, from the early 18th century onwards.

Marjorie, daughter of an accountant from Kirkcaldy, was an infant prodigy, producing diaries and essays as well as poems. Sir Walter Scott, a distant cousin, loved to hear her recite Shakespeare. "Marjorie! Marjorie! Where are ye, my bonnie wee croodlin doo?" he would (allegedly) cry on entering the house. I prefer the comment of her later champion, Mark Twain: "She was the world's child, she was the human race in little."

Marjorie died, probably of meningitis, before her ninth birthday.

3

COLOUR

U se of colour is as emotive for poets as it is for painters. It can be enriched with symbolic meaning, as
in Wilfrid Scawen Blunt's "reddest rose in all the world",
or part of the descriptive organisation, as with Edward
Thomas' black charcoal-burners, white linen and "naked
frosty blue" twilit sky. Each colour has a range of mood
and meaning; Padraic Colum uses blue as soothing,
almost numinous, while with characteristic daring D.H.
Lawrence enters into the heart of his blue gentians and
turns their darkness into a new kind of light.

Bavarian Gentians

BY D.H. LAWRENCE 1885–1930

Not every man has gentians in his house
in soft September, at slow, sad Michaelmas.

Bavarian gentians, big and dark, only dark
darkening the daytime torch-like with the smoking blueness
   of Pluto's gloom,
ribbed and torch-like, with their blaze of darkness spread
   blue
down flattening into points, flattened under the sweep of
   white day
torch-flower of the blue-smoking darkness, Pluto's dark-
   blue daze,
black lamps from the halls of Dis, burning dark blue,
giving off darkness, blue darkness, as Demeter's pale
   lamps give off light,
lead me then, lead me the way.

Reach me a gentian, give me a torch!
let me guide myself with the blue, forked torch of a flower
down the darker and darker stairs, where blue is
   darkened on blueness,

even where Persephone goes, just now, from the frosted
   September

to the sightless realm where darkness is awake upon the
   dark
and Persephone herself is but a voice
or a darkness invisible enfolded in the deeper dark
of the arms Plutonic, and pierced with the passion of
   dense gloom,
among the splendour of torches of darkness, shedding
darkness on the lost bride and her groom.

Lawrence wrote this a few months before he died of TB.
He uses the dark blue funnel-shaped flowers of the gentians brought to his sickbed by his wife as his imaginative entry to the underworld. Just as Persephone has to
leave the bright sunlit world every September to spend
the winter in Hades, the dark empire of her abductor-
husband Pluto, so Lawrence knows he must soon
descend the "darker and darker stairs". But he turns the
process inside out. Darkness becomes a different kind of
light, the gentian a torch "shedding darkness"; he seeks
some kind of control over his unavoidable fate – "let me
guide myself". And what awaits him is "splendour" and
"passion" in another form. "He wants death to be the
ultimate sexual experience," said Amanda. "He may be
dying, but he's the same old Lawrence."

Persephone's bargain was that after six months in darkness she would return to the surface, whereupon her mother Demeter could bring Spring to the earth. How can Lawrence emerge from the "sightless realm" of death? Only through his poetic voice. And it works. "The repetition of blue and dark is like an incantation," said Shelagh. "He draws us into his experience."

Juliet

BY WILFRID SCAWEN BLUNT 1840-1922

I see you, Juliet, still, with your straw hat
Loaded with vines, and with your dear pale face,
On which those thirty years so lightly sat,
And the white outline of your muslin dress.
You wore a little fichu trimmed with lace
And crossed in the front, as was the fashion then,
Bound at your waist with a broad band or sash,
All white and fresh and virginally plain.
There was a sound of shouting far away
Down in the valley, as they called to us,
And you, with hands clasped seeming still to pray
Patience of fate, stood listening to me thus
With heaving bosom. There a rose lay curled.
It was the reddest rose in all the world.

Look up Blunt online, and you'll be struck by an intense,
brooding face, strong-jawed, dark hair springing in a
thick wave. Atheist, though attracted by both Islam and
Roman Catholicism, anti-Imperialist, political prisoner,
saviour of the bloodline of Arab horses, it is no surprise

to find that he married Byron's granddaughter.

This sonnet comes from a sequence written about one of Blunt's several mistresses, possibly his cousin's wife Madeline Wyndham. Whoever "Juliet" was, in the poem she's real. This is a careful visual portrait. Blunt defines her by her clothes, in the way that Gainsborough or Reynolds or Manet defined their sitters by their clothes; he was a talented amateur artist, and it shows. He gives us a sensitive, passionate, suffering woman – a woman, not a girl; her "thirty years" is an important detail. At the volta – the turning point in a sonnet – we are momentarily distracted from our intense looking by listening; "they" ("so clever of him not to identify them", said Pepe) are shouting in the valley. Time is running out for the lovers.

I think I could do without the heaving bosom, but I forgive it for that perfect word "curled". The rose is Blake's "bed of crimson joy" ("The Sick Rose"), but undespoiled.

The Three Ravens

ANON., PUBLISHED 1611, PROBABLY OLDER

There were three ravens sat on a tree,
They were as black as they might be.

The one of them said to his mate,
"Where shall we our breakefast take?"

"Downe in yonder greene field,
There lies a knight slain under his shield.

"His hounds they lie downe at his feete,
So well they can their master keepe.

"His haukes they flie so eagerly,
There's no fowle dare come him nie."

Downe there comes a fallow doe,
As great with yong as she might goe.

She lift up his bloudy hed,
And kist his wounds that were so red.

She got him up upon her backe,
And carried him to earthen lake.

She buried him before the prime,
She was dead herselfe ere even-song time.

God send every gentleman,
Such haukes, such hounds, and such a leman.

As is usual with a traditional ballad, the story is simple but mysterious. The ravens have evil − or at least, breakfast − on their minds. They intend to eat the body of the knight, but he is protected by the fidelity of his hawks and hounds, and, as Clare felt, by nature itself; the greenness of the field is antithetical to the blackness of the ravens. The hawks and hounds keep scavengers off, but they make way for the pregnant doe. A third colour is introduced in the red of the wounds which the doe kisses before she gives the knight a decent burial. She is his "leman" (lover), presumably transformed by some enchantment into the shape of a deer, but this is not explained.

"It's great, the way you understand it on a level of feeling, not on a rational level," said Caroline T. Michael W said, "The wounds make you think of Christ, and the doe-woman has elements of the Virgin Mary and Mary Magdalen, but it avoids a complete parallel. The imaginative reach is breath-taking."

"Three ravens, three colours, three protective creatures. Is it something to do with the Holy Trinity?" suggested David. We concluded that chivalric Christian values were being presented symbolically or metaphorically.

Like "A Wooing Song of a Yeoman Of Kent's Son" (see page 112), this ballad was included by Thomas Ravenscroft in his *Melismata* in 1611. "The Twa Corbies", the Scottish variant, is much a darker story.

Jazzonia

BY LANGSTON HUGHES 1902–1967

Oh, silver tree!
Oh, shining rivers of the soul!

In a Harlem cabaret
Six long-headed jazzers play.
A dancing girl whose eyes are bold
Lifts high a dress of silken gold.

Oh, singing tree!
Oh, shining rivers of the soul!

Were Eve's eyes
In the first garden
Just a bit too bold?
Was Cleopatra gorgeous
In a gown of gold?

Oh, shining tree!
Oh, silver rivers of the soul!

In a whirling cabaret
Six long-headed jazzers play.

This is "Jazz poetry" from the Harlem Renaissance of the 1920s, the cultural movement created by black Americans who moved to New York to escape the institutionalised racism of the southern states. Langston Hughes wrote this at a time when black people were refused entry to smart jazz clubs, except as performers.

"For me, it's a celebration of the rhythm and freedom of jazz, of getting lost in music when sound and colour and movement fuse together," said Amanda. "And yet he's subtly appropriating Eve and Cleopatra – underneath there are echoes of a people being excluded from their own music."

Hughes was of mixed race; both paternal great-grandfathers were white slave-owners who impregnated their enslaved women. His lifelong championing of black Americans came from the influence of his maternal grandmother, who taught him to be proud of his racial heritage and to value its oral traditions.

A Cradle Song

BY PADRAIC COLUM 1881–1972

O men from the fields,
Come gently within.
Tread softly, softly
O men coming in!
Mavourneen is going
From me and from you,
Where Mary will fold him
With mantle of blue!
From reek of the smoke
And cold of the floor
And the peering of things
Across the half-door.
O men of the fields,
Soft, softly come thro'
Mary puts round him
Her mantle of blue.

This tender poem is a reverse nativity. In an Irish cabin, a baby is dying; "mavourneen" means "my darling" in Gaelic. Mary, mother of God, will shield him from the hardships of this life, the "reek of the smoke and cold of the floor". Her "mantle of blue" becomes both the essence of maternal love and the promise of Heaven. The "men of the fields" correspond to the shepherds paying homage to the Christ-child; the creatures "peering ... across the half-door" recall the ox and ass, though these "things" are a little more sinister than their scriptural equivalents. The dying child is treated with dignity, respect, adoring love. The gentle, lulling rhythm, the simple vocabulary, and the miraculous intensity of that "blue" make this a rare example of a poem on the death of a child that might actually console.

A Penny Whistle

BY EDWARD THOMAS 1878–1917

The new moon hangs like an ivory bugle
In the naked frosty blue;
And the ghylls of the forest, already blackened
By Winter, are blackened anew.

The brooks that cut up and increase the forest,
As if they had never known
The sun, are roaring with black hollow voices
Betwixt rage and a moan.

But still the caravan-hut by the hollies
Like a kingfisher gleams between:
Round the mossed old hearths of the charcoal-burners
First primroses ask to be seen.

The charcoal-burners are black, but their linen
Blows white on the line;
And white the letter the girl is reading
Under that crescent fine;

And her brother who hides apart in a thicket,
Slowly and surely playing
On a whistle an old nursery melody,
Says far more than I am saying.

The scene is painterly but precise, pared down, black-white-blue. Nature is harsh, as are the lives of the itinerant charcoal-burners, so close to the elements. Charcoal-burners, with their permanently blackened faces and isolated woodland existence, were often feared, suspected of dark practices. But for Edward Thomas their return each year to their "mossed old hearths" makes them as much a part of the cycle of renewal as the first primroses.

Human impulse towards art as a way of elevating and shaping life is evident in the pure, simple tune coming from the thicket. The eye is led to the white spot of the letter which holds all the hopes and desires of the girl ("as if it's in a Vermeer painting", said Michael W, a painter himself); her brother's penny whistle, the equivalent of the moon's "ivory bugle", shapes the moment for Edward Thomas, and in turn his poem does the same for us.

"This poem triggered a brief state of utter stillness, contentment and well-being," said Caroline T. "I find that this type of experience cannot be predicted or grasped; I suspect it involves a connection with something universal and so mysteriously comforting, whether the feelings involved are positive or negative."

Silent Noon

BY DANTE GABRIEL ROSSETTI, 1828–1882

Your hands lie open in the long fresh grass, –
The finger-points look through like rosy blooms:
Your eyes smile peace. The pasture gleams and glooms
'Neath billowing skies that scatter and amass.
All round our nest, far as the eye can pass,
Are golden kingcup fields with silver edge
Where the cow-parsley skirts the hawthorn-hedge.
'Tis visible silence, still as the hour-glass.

Deep in the sun-searched growths the dragon-fly
Hangs like a blue thread loosened from the sky: –
So this wing'd hour is dropt to us from above.
Oh! clasp we to our hearts, for deathless dower,
This close-companioned inarticulate hour
When two-fold silence was the song of love.

This sonnet, from Rossetti's sequence *The House of Life*,
is about Lizzie Siddal, his muse, mistress, and (eventually) his wife. Lizzie, a talented artist in her own right,
modelled for Rossetti but also for other Pre-Raphaelite

painters; most famously she was Millais' slow-drowning Ophelia. Her relationship with Rossetti was rarely less than fraught; "Silent Noon" captures a rare moment of shared peace.

Rossetti described the sonnet form as "a moment's monument". This intense, absorbingly visual poem fulfils exactly that function. The colours, made special by the emotion of the moment, create "visible silence"; her rosy fingertips, the silvery cow parsley, and, most memorably, the "blue thread" of the dragon-fly connecting earth and heaven. "That is exactly what dragon-flies are like!" exclaimed Sarah N with satisfaction.

It couldn't last. In 1862 Lizzie died, probably of a deliberate overdose, after giving birth to their stillborn child. Rossetti buried his poems with her, including this one. He entwined them in her beautiful golden hair.

Seven years later, it occurred to both Rossetti and his agent Charles Howell that this was a bit of a waste. Howell ordered a midnight exhumation. The sodden, worm-bored manuscript was taken away to be disinfected and was then returned to Rossetti. The salvaged poems were included in his influential volume, simply entitled *Poems*, published the following year, which incorporated verses addressed to his next great love, his friend William Morris' wife Jane. "Not his finest hour," said Pam.

The story of the exhumation was not generally known until after Rossetti's own death in 1882. Howell's account included the fanciful claim that Lizzie's disinterred body was "perfect", which led to the myth that her hair had grown to fill the coffin like spun gold. I prefer the living gold of the kingcups in "Silent Noon" which was set to music by Ralph Vaughan Williams.

Home From Abroad

BY LAURIE LEE 1914–1997

Far-fetched with tales of other worlds and ways,
My skin well-oiled with wines of the Levant,
I set my face into a filial smile
To greet the pale, domestic kiss of Kent.

But shall I never learn? That gawky girl,
Recalled so primly in my foreign thoughts,
Becomes again the green-haired queen of love
Whose wanton form dilates as it delights.

Her rolling tidal landscape floods the eye
And drowns Chianti in a dusky stream;
The flower-decked grasses swim with simple horses,
The hedges choke with roses fat as cream.

So do I breathe the hayblown airs of home,
And watch the sea-green elms drip birds and shadows,
And as the twilight nets the plunging sun
My heart's keel slides to rest among the meadows.

Pam brought this one in; she has always relished the juiciness of Laurie Lee. Veronica loved the way Lee merges land and ocean in rolling movement. Kent – the first county reached on returning from the continent – metamorphoses from a predictably unemphatic and unexciting mother presenting a dry, shore-bound cheek for a "domestic" kiss into a water goddess, half Venus, half siren. In her domain, horses swim in the meadows, elms move like giant seaweed. The setting sun is caught as in a fishing net, and Lee's heart finds its harbour. This sumptuous evocation of an almost erotic response to a homeland feels so colourful that it's a surprise to find that there are only two colours in it, cream and green (unless you stretch to include "pale" and "dusky"). But, like a true poet, Lee makes his "green" more than a colour. It becomes a sensuous, immersive imaginative experience.

4

LOVERS, COURTSHIP & SEDUCTION

The pains and pleasures of love are, of course, the very stuff of poetry – this is the heart of the human story. All the poems in this section involve movement – chasing, dancing, travelling, swimming, flying – because desire is what makes things happen.

Tuscan Olives (rispetti)

BY AGNES MARY FRANCES ROBINSON DARMESTETER
DUCLAUX 1857–1944

The colour of the olives who shall say?
In winter on the yellow earth they're blue,
A wind can change the green to white or gray,
But they are olives still in every hue:
But they are olives always, green or white.
As love is love in torment or delight;
But they are olives, ruffled or at rest,
As love is always love in tears or jest.

We walked along the terraced olive-yard,
And talked together till we lost the way;
We met a peasant, bent with age, and hard,
Bruising the grape-skins in a vase of clay;
Bruising the grape-skins for the second wine.
We did not drink, and left him, Love of mine,
Bruising the grapes already bruised enough:
He had his meagre wine, and we our love.

We climbed one morning to the sunny height,
Where chestnuts grow no more, and olives grow;
Far-off the circling mountains, cinder-white,
The yellow river and the gorge below.
"Turn round," you said, O flower of Paradise;
I did not turn, I looked upon your eyes.

"Turn round," you said, "turn round, look at the view!"
I did not turn, my Love. I looked at you.

How hot it was! Across the white-hot wall
Pale olives stretch towards the blazing street;
You broke a branch, you never spoke at all,
But gave it me to fan with in the heat;
You gave it me without a word or sign:
Under the olives first I called you mine.

At Lucca, for the autumn festival,
The streets are tulip-gay; but you and I
Forget them, seeing over church and wall
Guinigi's tower soar i' the black-blue sky,
A stem of delicate rose against the blue,
And on the top two lonely olives grew,
Crowning the tower, far from the hills, alone,
As on our risen love our lives are grown.

Who would have thought we should stand again together,
Here, with the convent a frown of towers above us;
Here, mid the sere-wooded hills and wintry weather;
Here, where the olives bend down and seem to love us;
Here, where the fruit-laden olives half remember
All that began in their shadow last November;
Here, where we knew we must part, must part and sever;
Here where we know we shall love aye and ever.

Reach up and pluck a branch, and give it me,
That I may hang it in my Northern room,
That I may find it there, and wake, and see
– Not you! not you! – dead leaves and wintry gloom.
O senseless olives, wherefore should I take
Your leaves to balm a heart that can but ache?
Why should I take you hence, that can but show
How much is left behind? I do not know.

Rispetti sound like delicious little biscuits, but actually
they're Italian verse stanzas, six to ten lines long, with
rhymes. Mary Robinson (let's boil her six names down to
two) chose an Italian form for the Italian setting of this
poem of love and landscape. In 1880 she was travelling
in Italy when she met Violet Paget, a writer of supernatural fiction who used the pseudonym Vernon Lee – she
was the half-sister of Eugene Lee-Hamilton (see page 50).
"Tuscan Olives" tells how the two women fell in love.

It's painterly; the olive trees blue against the yellow
winter earth, the cinder-white mountains, the rose-
pink spire against the black-blue sky. It's also rich with
symbolism. Olives remain olives despite their changing
appearance, and love is love "in torment or delight",
but perhaps there's another layer, a hint at the necessary

disguises these women adopt in order to express their true selves. Talking hard, they lose their way, but it's a way that needs to be lost if they are to find what they really want. They leave the hard old man mistreating the grapes behind them, and move into their own sphere, a charmed circle within which they enact their own love ritual. Violet presents Mary with an olive branch, as if to a deity in the ancient world. The olive is a sacred tree, symbolising abundance, glory, wisdom, peace and victory. It is the emblem of the goddess Athena.

Months later, ignoring the bustle of the autumn festival, the mainstream life that is not for them, they see their love symbolised by two olive trees growing on the top of the tower, high above the town, lonely but glorious, "crowning". The convent and all it represents may frown above them, and they must separate, but having declared their love here they are part of this landscape. The olives that "bend down and seem to love" them have borne fruit.

It seems to be a poem about the triumph of love, but suddenly the mood turns. Mary asks Violet to pick her another branch, to hang in her room back in chilly London. But even as she asks, she realises that symbols aren't the real thing. Just as, at the blazing-hot heart of the poem, she looked, not at the view but straight at Violet, her "flower of Paradise", so now she knows that waking alone and looking at a withered branch won't help. "Not you! not you!" is the desolate inverse of the erotic "I looked at you" of the third rispetto.

Mary lived and travelled with Violet/Vernon in Europe for eight years, during which time she wrote the first full-length biography of Emily Brontë. In 1888 she married, abruptly, Professor Darmesteter, a French Jew. Poor Violet had a breakdown.

One of the group brought in a portrait of Violet by John Singer Sargent. Violet was responsible for introducing the concept of empathy into the study of aesthetics, and one could see this in her kind and lively face. However, she didn't fit anyone's idea of a "flower of Paradise". Beauty, we agreed, is in the eye of the beholder.

Eve

BY RALPH HODGSON 1871–1962

Eve, with her basket, was
Deep in the bells and grass,
Wading in bells and grass
Up to her knees,
Picking a dish of sweet
Berries and plums to eat,
Down in the bells and grass
Under the trees.

Mute as a mouse in a
Corner the cobra lay,
Curled round a bough of the
Cinnamon tall...
Now to get even and
Humble proud heaven and –
Now was the moment or
Never at all.

"Eva!" Each syllable
Light as a flower fell,
"Eva!" he whispered the
Wondering maid,
Soft as a bubble sung
Out of a linnet's lung,
Soft and most silverly
"Eva!" he said.

Picture that orchard sprite,
Eve, with her body white,
Supple and smooth to her
Slim finger tips,
Wondering, listening,
Listening, wondering,
Eve with a berry
Half-way to her lips.

Oh, had our simple Eve
Seen through the make-believe!
Had she but known the
Pretender he was!
Out of the boughs he came,
Whispering still her name,
Tumbling in twenty rings
Into the grass.

Here was the strangest pair
In the world anywhere,
Eve in the bells and grass
Kneeling, and he
Telling his story low...
Singing birds saw them go
Down the dark path to
The Blasphemous Tree.

Oh, what a clatter when
Titmouse and Jenny Wren
Saw him successful and
Taking his leave!
How the birds rated him!
How they all hated him!
How they all pitied
Poor motherless Eve!

Picture her crying,
Outside in the lane,
Eve, with no dish of sweet
Berries and plums to eat,
Haunting the gate of the
Orchard in vain...
Picture that lewd delight
Under the hill to-night –
"Eva!" the toast goes round,
"Eva!" again.

"Oh, Evewithherbasketwas!" exclaimed Pepe. "I painted a picture of her when I was at school. I don't think I've read the poem since." Indeed, it is a strongly visual poem. Ralph Hodgson twice asks us to "picture" Eve; once before her fall when she's an "orchard sprite", a deeply sensuous and desirable one with a berry provocatively "half-way to her lips", then again after her expulsion from Paradise, "crying outside in the lane". In one fluid movement, as sinuous as the snake itself, Hodgson has transformed Eve from a half-mythical being into a contemporary servant girl, a Hardyesque "ruined maid", her seduction gloated over by the all-too-human serpent and his drinking companions.

"It's that rhythm," said David, "it's a seduction in itself." Hodgson uses dactyls, since you ask – *dum*diddy *dum*diddy, a rhythm containing its own miniature falls.

The Dalliance of the Eagles

BY WALT WHITMAN 1819–1892

Skirting the river road, (my forenoon walk, my rest,)
Skyward in air a sudden muffled sound, the dalliance
    of the eagles,
The rushing amorous contact high in space together,
The clinching interlocking claws, a living, fierce,
    gyrating wheel,
Four beating wings, two beaks, a swirling mass tight
    grappling,
In tumbling turning clustering loops, straight
    downward falling,
Till o'er the river pois'd, the twain yet one, a moment's
    lull,
A motionless still balance in the air, then parting,
    talons loosing,
Upward again on slow-firm pinions slanting, their
    separate diverse flight,
She hers, he his, pursuing.

"How interesting that there's no main verb," said Shelagh. Whitman's rushing "ing" endings keep the eagles aloft, and then there's that moment of consummation, "a motionless still balance".

"It's wonderfully alive," said Sarah N, "because he's identifying with them so closely, and yet keeping them as real eagles."

Sonnet 190

BY PETRARCH 1304–1374

Una candida cerva sopra l'erba
verde m'apparve, con duo corna d'oro,
fra due riviere, all'ombra d'un alloro,
levando 'l sole a la stagione acerba.

Era sua vista si dolce superba,
ch'i' lasciai per seguirla ogni lavoro:
come l'avaro che 'n cercar tesoro
con diletto l'affanno disacerba.

"Nessun mi tocchi – al bel collo d'intorno
scritto avea di diamanti et di topazi –;
libera farmi al mio Cesare parve."

Et era 'l sol già volto al mezzo giorno,
gli occhi miei stanchi di mirar, non sazi,
quand'io caddi ne l'acqua, et ella sparve.

Sonnet 190
MY VERSION

A white hind with two golden horns
appeared to me on the green grass
between two rivers, in the shade of a laurel,
as the sun rose in the green springtime.

She looked so gentle, so magnificent,
that I downed tools to follow only her:
so the miser's joy in the search for treasure
softens the hardship of his quest.

"Do not touch me" – round her lovely neck
this was written in topaz and in diamonds:
"My Lord has seen fit to set me free".

Already the sun had jumped to noon,
my eyes were gaze-weary, but not sated,
when I slid into the water, and she vanished.

and WHOSO LIST TO HUNT

BY SIR THOMAS WYATT 1503-1542

Whoso list to hunt, I know where is an hind,
But as for me, *hélas*, I may no more.
The vain travail hath wearied me so sore,
I am of them that farthest cometh behind.
Yet may I by no means my wearied mind
Draw from the deer, but as she fleeth afore
Fainting I follow. I leave off therefore,
Sithens in a net I seek to hold the wind.
Who list her hunt, I put him out of doubt,
As well as I may spend his time in vain.
And graven with diamonds in letters plain
There is written her fair neck round about:
"*Noli me tangere*, for Caesar's I am,
And wild for to hold, though I seem tame."

Wyatt and his friend Henry Howard, Earl of Surrey (see
page 245) were responsible for bringing sonnets into the
English language. Petrarch was the great Italian sonne-
teer, and Wyatt, Surrey and their followers usually stuck
to the line length and rhyme scheme of the Petrarchan

model. But their imitations were never slavish, their translations never literal. Petrarch's Sonnet 190 describes a vision, a mystical equivalent of his desire for his idealised love object, the beautiful, but dead, Laura (whose name slips into the poem in the form of the laurel tree). Michael W, who knows some Italian, read it aloud; we could pick up the mood of slow dreaminess, the feeling of something just out of reach.

Wyatt's version isn't dreamy at all. It's tense, febrile, fast and yet effortful. The legend is that Wyatt's "hind" (no longer pure white) is Anne Boleyn, at this point being pursued by many courtiers, but most importantly by Henry VIII, and I really don't want any scholarly researcher to disabuse me of this thrilling story. When, a couple of years later, Anne fell from favour, Wyatt was one of many accused of adultery with her. He was imprisoned in the Tower of London; from the window of his cell he witnessed the execution of his fellow prisoners, possibly even that of Anne herself. "These bloody days have broken my heart... The bell-tower showed me such sight/That in my head sticks day and night," he wrote. He was himself acquitted.

This poem belongs to an earlier period, when the chase is still on, though Wyatt can't keep up – "I am of them that farthest cometh behind"; can't keep up, but can't *give* up either, because he's under the spell, not only of Anne's allure, but of the whole courtly game. Petrarch's "eyes were gaze-weary, but not sated"; with

Wyatt, this becomes "Yet may I by no means my wearied mind/Draw from the deer". Psychologically, mind is an intriguing exchange for eyes.

Petrarch's sentences move smoothly to a full stop at the end of each section, a long pause for reflection. Wyatt throws a remarkable full stop right into the middle of his sonnet: "Fainting I follow. I leave off therefore"; the repeated Fs imitate panting, and the full stop enacts his despairing stumble. Shelagh particularly admired the desolate beauty of the next line, "Sithens [since] in a net I seek to hold the wind".

Then there's the jewelled collar encircling the neck of the lovely creature. Petrarch's diamonds and topaz harmonise with the white of the hind and the gold of her horns. Wyatt leaves out the topaz, and gives us only the hard dazzle of the diamonds. "Graven" is a strong word, almost painful. The diamonds make up the "letters plain", but diamonds are also used for gouging words onto glass, and the word "grave" carries its own sombre weight; altogether "graven" packs more of a punch than Petrarch's more everyday "scritto".

And what of the message itself? "Noli me tangere", don't touch me – the words spoken by the risen Christ to Mary Magdalen outside his empty tomb. Petrarch puts the words into his native Italian, "Nessun mi tocchi", which seems gentler. Wyatt's Latin stands out like a prickly hedge, or like William Blake's " 'Thou shalt not' writ over the door" in "The Garden of Love".

Petrarch's hind is controlled by her "Cesare", out of Petrarch's reach, but the control seems benevolent, akin to the worship of God "whose service is perfect freedom". Laura, whom the hind represents, is already dead; the poem is a vision of another world than this. Wyatt's hind is very much alive. The Anne Boleyn message crackles with ambivalence. "And wild for to hold, though I seem tame" – does Henry/Caesar know what he's letting himself in for? This deer-woman is fully aware of her own power.

When we think of Anne Boleyn, we unavoidably think of her neck. Wyatt's lines seem prescient; in time, this Caesar will replace the diamonds with the shining edge of a silver sword. But I can't attribute clairvoyance to Wyatt, much though I'd like to round off the myth with it.

"This poem is politically incorrect on every level," said Cresta. "Hunting deer, stalking women... but it reaches across five hundred years to describe passion and unrequited love. It's extraordinarily powerful to think of Thomas Wyatt desperate for a woman he can't touch."

Indoor Games Near Newbury

BY JOHN BETJEMAN 1906–1984

In among the silver birches winding ways of tarmac
    wander
And the signs to Bussock Bottom, Tussock Wood and
    Windy Break,
Gabled lodges, tile-hung churches, catch the lights of
    our Lagonda
As we drive to Wendy's party, lemon curd and
    Christmas cake.
        Rich the makes of motor whirring,
        Past the pine plantation purring
           Come up, Hupmobile, Delage!
        Short the way your chauffeurs travel,
        Crunching over private gravel
        Each from out his warm garage.

O but Wendy, when the carpet yielded to my indoor
    pumps
There you stood, your gold hair streaming,
Handsome in the hall-light gleaming
There you looked and there you led me off into the
    game of clumps
        Then the new Victrola playing
        And your funny uncle saying
"Choose your partners for a foxtrot! Dance until it's tea
    o'clock!

"Come on, young 'uns, foot it featly!"
Was it chance that paired us neatly,
I, who loved you so completely,
You, who pressed me closely to you, hard against your
party frock?

"Meet me when you've finished eating!" So we met
and no one found us.
Oh that dark and furry cupboard while the rest played
hide-and-seek!
Holding hands our two hearts beating in the bedroom
silence round us,
Holding hands and hardly hearing sudden footstep,
thud and shriek.
Love that lay too deep for kissing –
"Where is Wendy? Wendy's missing!"
Love so pure it *had* to end,
Love so strong that I was frighten'd
When you gripped my fingers tight and
Hugging, whispered "I'm your friend."

Good-bye Wendy! Send the fairies, pinewood elf and
larch tree gnome,
Spingle-spangled stars are peeping
At the lush Lagonda creeping
Down the winding ways of tarmac to the leaded lights
of home.
There, among the silver birches,

All the bells of all the churches
Sounded in the bath-waste running out into the frosty air.
Wendy speeded my undressing,
Wendy is the sheet's caressing
Wendy bending gives a blessing,
Holds me as I drift to dreamland, safe inside my
slumber wear.

Betjeman had a genius for specificity. Through the details of affluent Home Counties interwar transport, furnishings, food and clothes, he makes the ardour of first love warm and real to us. He's the master of bathos, but it's not scornful or reductive; "There, among the silver birches/ All the bells of all the churches/ Sounded in the bath-waste running out into the frosty air" perfectly expresses how the boy's emotional excitement pervades everything in his world.

We know we can rely on Betjeman to get things right. "Hupmobile, Delage" – these luxurious cars belong only to this period. New money, new luxuries – even the tree-planting is a little vulgar, but the feelings are real. Young love blossoming in the "dark and furry cupboard" – "He's so good at texture," said Sarah N.

"This is the best kind of nostalgia," said Amanda.

A Wooing Song of a Yeoman of Kent's Son

ANON., FROM MELISMATA, 1611

I have house and land in Kent,
And if you'll love me, love me now;
Twopence-halfpenny is my rent,
I cannot come every day to woo.

I am my father's eldest son,
My mother eke doth love me well,
For I can bravely clout my shoon,
And I full well can ring a bell.

My father he gave me a hog,
My mother she gave me a sow;
I have a God-father dwells thereby,
And he on me bestowed a plow.

One time I gave thee a paper of pins,
Another time a tawdry-lace;
And if thou wilt not grant me love,
In truth I die before thy face.

I have been twice our Whitsun-lord,
I have had ladies many fair,
And eke thou hast my heart in hold
And in my mind seems passing rare.

I will put on my best white slops
And I will wear my yellow hose,
And on my head a good grey hat,
And in't I stick a lovely rose.

Wherefore cease off, make no delay,
And if you'll love me, love me now
Or else I seek some otherwhere,
For I cannot come every day to woo.

[bravely = expertly; clout my shoon = mend or patch my shoes; tawdry-lace = a ribbon worn as a necklace, as sold at Saint Audrey's Fair; Whitsun-lord = leader of the village youth for the Whitsun festivities, so the male equivalent of the May Queen; slops = breeches]

Poetry (or perhaps verse would be a better word in this case) opens doors through which we can step into the past. The Yeoman's Son is as vivid as one of Chaucer's pilgrims or Shakespeare's rustics, and continues to pop up in modern form on TV dating shows. He comes to us courtesy of a composer and music theorist called

Thomas Ravenscroft (1588–1635) who collected and published the "anonymous music" of the Jacobean age – street cries, vendor songs, ballads, nursery rhymes, catches and rounds. "Three Blind Mice" comes to us via Ravenscroft. So does the ballad "The Three Ravens" (see page 75).

This could be classed as a vendor song, the Yeoman's Son doing his best to sell himself. "At least she knows what she's getting," said Pepe. "I find him resistible," said Shelagh.

The Farmer's Bride

BY CHARLOTTE MEW 1869–1928

Three summers since I chose a maid,
    Too young maybe – but more's to do
At harvest-time than bide and woo.
       When us was wed she turned afraid
Of love and me and all things human;
Like the shut of a winter's day
Her smile went out, and 'twadn't a woman –
     More like a little frightened fay.
         One night, in the Fall, she runned away.

"Out 'mong the sheep, her be," they said,
'Should properly have been abed;
But sure enough she wadn't there
Lying awake with her wide brown stare.
So over seven-acre field and up-along across the down
    We chased her, flying like a hare
Before our lanterns. To Church-Town
      All in a shiver and a scare
We caught her, fetched her home at last
      And turned the key upon her, fast.

She does the work about the house
As well as most, but like a mouse:
      Happy enough to chat and play

With birds and rabbits and such as they,
So long as men-folk keep away.
"Not near, not near!" her eyes beseech
When one of us comes within reach.
The women say that beasts in stall
Look round like children at her call.
I've hardly heard her speak at all.

Shy as a leveret, swift as he,
Straight and slight as a young larch tree,
Sweet as the first wild violets, she,
To her wild self. But what to me?

The short days shorten and the oaks are brown,
The blue smoke rises to the low grey sky,
One leaf in the still air falls slowly down,
A magpie's spotted feathers lie
On the black earth spread white with rime,
The berries redden up to Christmas-time.
What's Christmas-time without there be
Some other in the house than we!

She sleeps up in the attic there
Alone, poor maid. 'Tis but a stair
Betwixt us. Oh! my God! the down,
The soft young down of her, the brown,
The brown of her – her eyes, her hair, her hair!

"You really feel for both of them," said Pepe, "that's the clever thing. It would be too easy to make him simply the abuser, but he doesn't go up the stairs to the attic. He longs for her to come to him, but it's not going to happen."

"It's the tragic inverse of the Yeoman of Kent's Son," said Clare.

Charlotte Mew's own story is unbearably sad. Her architect father died leaving no financial provision; three of the children died in childhood, two others were committed to mental asylums. The remaining two, Charlotte and her sister Anne, lived together in poverty, and made a pact never to marry for fear of passing on the "family taint". In any case, marriage would hardly have suited Charlotte, whose romantic feelings were directed at women. She cut her hair short, dressed "like a dandy", and often wrote from the point of view of a male protagonist, as she does in "The Farmer's Bride".

Charlotte's poems and stories were published in magazines and were admired by writers as diverse as Thomas Hardy, Siegfried Sassoon and Virginia Woolf; in Woolf's opinion she was "very good and interesting and quite unlike anybody else". Hardy, John Masefield, Walter de la Mare and the museum curator Sydney Cockerell got together to organise a pension for her, which helped.

But when Anne died of cancer, the long-dreaded mental illness struck. Racked with irrational anxiety that she had caused her sister to be buried alive, Charlotte went into an asylum, where she killed herself by drinking Lysol.

Her subtle poems use a wide variety of styles – some are startlingly modernist – and show a particular affinity with people living on the edge of society.

Homely Meats

BY JOHN DAVIES OF HEREFORD C.1565–1618

The author loving these homely meats specially, viz.: cream, pan-cakes, buttered pippin-pies (laugh, good people) and tobacco; writ to that worthy and virtuous gentlewoman, whom he calleth Mistress, as followeth:

If there were, oh! an Hellespont of cream
Between us, milk-white mistress, I would swim
To you, to show to both my love's extreme,
Leander-like, – yea! dive from brim to brim.
But met I with a buttered pippin-pie
Floating upon 't, that would I make my boat
To waft me to you without jeopardy,
Though sea-sick I might be while it did float.
Yet if a storm should rise, by night or day,
Of sugar-snows and hail of caraways,
Then, if I found a pancake in my ways,
It like a plank should bring me to your kays;
Which having found, if they tobacco kept,
The smoke should dry me well before I slept.

"How lovely to have a poem about food!" said Pepe. And what charmingly turn-of-the-17th-century food, too. Pippin-pies, sugar-snows, caraways, and a nice solid pancake to bring the cream-swimmer safe to port. It's interesting that newly–discovered tobacco is categorised as a foodstuff.

If you think you've spotted a sexual reference or two, you're probably right. John Davies was a friend of John Donne, who was not averse to a double entendre; "Homely Meats" is as sexual as you want it to be.

Davies was a handwriting expert and taught penmanship to Prince Henry, eldest son of James I. He knew Shakespeare, Sidney and Ben Jonson, and may even be the author of "A Lover's Complaint", which is usually attributed to Shakespeare. He settled in Oxford, but called himself "John Davies of Hereford" partly to distinguish himself from Sir John Davies, another poet, and partly because he was proud and fond of his birthplace, the ancient town on the banks of the Wye.

5

MYSTERY & ENCHANTMENT

Magic is where my love of poetry began, in early childhood. Perhaps it's where all poetry truly begins, with the power of the incantation. For a spell to work, you must get the pattern exactly right, and poetry is patterned language. The poet – even the playground rhyme-maker – believes in the reality of the imagination; combine this with the power of pattern-making, and you have a formula which transports you into the realms of mysterious enchantment other art forms cannot reach.

The Hag

BY ROBERT HERRICK 1591–1674

The hag is astride,
This night for to ride;
The Devill and shee together:
Through thick, and through thin,
Now out, and then in,
Though ne'er so foul be the weather.

A Thorn or a Burr
She takes for a Spurre:
With a lash of a Bramble she rides now,
Through Brakes and through Bryars,
O'er Ditches, and Mires,
She followes the Spirit that guides now.

No Beast, for his food,
Dares now range the wood;
But husht in his laire he lies lurking:
While mischiefs, by these,
On Land and on Seas,
At noone of Night are a-working.

The storme will arise,
And trouble the skies;
This night, and more for the wonder,

The ghost from the Tomb
Affrighted shall come,
Call'd out by the clap of the Thunder.

This thrilled me as a child. The heart-thump rhythm, the sense of immediacy, booming rhymes like "wonder" and "Thunder" – the poem carried me through the troubled skies in the wake of the hag and the devil. "Spurre", "lash", "mires", "lurking", "mischiefs", "noone of Night", "Tomb" – the vocabulary was delightfully frightening. My older brother's birthday was (is) on Hallowe'en, and in my young imagination this was one of the most interesting days of the year.

Robert Herrick, vicar of Dean Prior in deepest, darkest 17th-century Devon, wrote literally thousands of poems in which he juicily combined his literary and classical knowledge (he was a graduate of Cambridge and a friend and follower of Ben Jonson) with the folklore, customs and superstitions of his parishioners. "The Hag" is often included in anthologies for children, but for the adult inhabitants of Dean Prior, perhaps for Herrick himself, witches were real. The hag's out there right now, this very night, and she's unstoppable.

When we read this poem it provoked the interesting

revelation that one of those present had belonged to a coven. She shall remain nameless.

For a sympathetic portrayal of the very appealing Herrick, and for more on witches, see Rose Macaulay's Civil War novel, *They Were Defeated*.

The Song of the Mad Prince

BY WALTER DE LA MARE 1873–1956

Who said, "Peacock Pie?"
The old King to the sparrow:
Who said, "Crops are ripe"?
Rust to the harrow:
Who said, "Where sleeps she now?
Where rests she now her head,
Bathed in eve's loveliness"? –
That's what I said.

Who said, "Ay, mum's the word"?
Sexton to willow:
Who said, "Green dusk for dreams,
Moss for a pillow"?
Who said, "All Time's delight
Hath she for narrow bed;
Life's troubled bubble broken"? –
That's what I said.

Walter de la Mare is one of those rare poets who writes
equally well for children and for adults. I first encoun-

tered "The Song of the Mad Prince" when I was seven or eight. I remember sitting on my Aunt Hilary's bedroom windowsill, reading it aloud to her, feeling it throb with ungraspable significance. It was in de la Mare's children's collection *Peacock Pie*, first published in 1913 – indeed, the collection takes its title from this poem. Edward Ardizzone's shadowy, suggestive illustrations perfectly complemented de la Mare's talent for creating a profound sense of mystery in very few words.

Five decades later, the Mad Prince's appeal is as strong for me as ever. There are tasting notes of *Hamlet* – the sexton, the willow, the dead girl, the concealment of dark deeds, the prince himself – but the story is de la Mare's own. Or rather, it is the reader's own. "There are five questions," said Olivia, "but none of them are asked by one human to another." The answers are buried in the girl's mossy grave. What we make of it depends on which doors it opens in our individual imaginations.

How does de la Mare make a simple word like "rust" seem so long, so resonant, so important? The ability to do so makes him a true poet.

"Walter de la Mare's 'The Listeners' was the first poem of my choice in my early teens," said Veronica, and Pam remembered it from her teaching days as the poem most likely to win a class over to poetry.

The Cherry Tree Carol

ANON., C. 15TH CENTURY

Joseph was an old man, and an old man was he,
when he wedded Mary in the land of Galilee.

Joseph and Mary walk'd through an orchard good,
where was cherries and berries so red as any blood.

Joseph and Mary walk'd through an orchard green,
where was berries and cherries as thick as might be seen.

O then bespoke Mary, so meek and so mild,
"Pluck me one cherry, Joseph, for I am with child."

O then bespoke Joseph with words so unkind,
"Let him pluck thee a cherry that brought thee with
    child."

O then bespoke the babe within his mother's womb,
  "Bow down then the tallest tree for my mother to have
    some."

Then bow'd down the highest tree unto his mother's
    hand:
when she cried, "See, Joseph, I have cherries at
    command!"

O then bespake Joseph – "I have done Mary wrong;
but cheer up, my dearest, and be not cast down.

"O eat your cherries, Mary, O eat your cherries now;
O eat your cherries, Mary, that grow upon the bough."

Then Mary pluck'd a cherry as red as the blood;
then Mary went home with her heavy load.

Then Mary took her young son and set him on her knee,
"I pray thee now, dear child, tell how this world shall be."

"O I shall be as dead, mother, as the stones in the wall;
O the stones in the street, mother, shall mourn for me all.

"And upon a Wednesday my vow I will make,
and upon Good Friday my death will I take.

"Upon Easter-day, mother, my uprising shall be,
O the sun and the moon, mother, shall both rise with
  me!"

This charming ballad, which appears in the "N-Town"
Mystery Plays performed in the English Midlands

around 1500, may have its roots in the "dialogue hymns" of early medieval Syriac liturgy, perhaps brought to England by crusader knights returning from the Holy Land in the 12th and 13th centuries. The story comes from the apocryphal "Gospel of Pseudo-Matthew", but has been made more English, more domestic and more psychologically real. In Pseudo-Matthew, it's a date palm, not a cherry tree, and Joseph speaks no unkind words to Mary. But to us, Joseph's grumpy "Let him pluck thee a cherry that brought thee with child" is believably human. "I like the way he's so definite about the days of the week," said Mike F.

Mary reverses the sin of Eve in tempting Adam to eat the forbidden fruit. The holy child in her womb licenses her eating of the cherries. But still they bring a burden of knowledge – "O I shall be as dead, mother, as the stones in the wall."

"What intrigues me about the older poems," said Shelagh, "is the entertainment or performance aspect. Bards and storytellers would have gathered people round fires after the day's work or on festive occasions. The poems would have reinforced identities and shared values, and for a largely illiterate audience the rhymes and rhythms and structures would have helped memory and oral transmission. They must have undergone many transformations before anyone committed them to paper."

"Shakespeare would have known poems like this, they

are part of our heritage," said Polly. "Medieval poetry is so very moving and the basis of all our later poetry."

"Polly is so right!" said Veronica. "If someone like me, with not much literary background, can become involved with the rhythm and the sound, how can they be abandoned?"

Fairy Story

BY STEVIE SMITH 1902–1971

I went into the wood one day
And there I walked and lost my way

When it was so dark I could not see
A little creature came to me

He said if I could sing a song
The time would not be very long

But first I must let him hold my hand tight
Or else the wood would give me a fright

I sang a song, he let me go
But now I am home again there is nobody I know.

The almost clumsy simplicity is as deceptive as the little creature himself. This small poem gets to the core of psychological alienation. "Something happened to her that changed everything for ever," said Judith. Stevie Smith, aged five, contracted tubercular peritonitis and was committed to a hospital where she spent the next three years, so it's tempting to link the poem to this experience. But even without this information you can taste the fear. Clare said, "It's a near-nursery rhyme, a simple verse, and yet it never ceases to upend that simplicity. Its sinister magic opens the possibilities to other worlds with its feeling of the uncanny. It catches people off guard as its strangeness seeps in."

Roe-Deer

BY TED HUGHES 1930–1998

In the dawn-dirty light, in the biggest snow of the year
Two blue-dark deer stood in the road, alerted.

They had happened into my dimension
The moment I was arriving just there.

They planted their two or three years of secret deerhood
Clear on my snow-screen vision of the abnormal

And hesitated in the all-way disintegration
And stared at me. And so for some lasting seconds

I could think the deer were waiting for me
To remember the password and sign

That the curtain had blown aside for a moment
And there where the trees were no longer trees, nor
   the road a road

The deer had come for me.

Then they ducked through the hedge, and upright
   they rode their legs
Away downhill over a snow-lonely field

Towards tree dark – finally
Seeming to eddy and glide and fly away up

Into the boil of big flakes.
The snow took them and soon their nearby hoofprints
    as well

Revising its dawn inspiration
Back to the ordinary.

This was David's choice. He writes poetry himself; like most poets, or artists of any kind, in his work he's in search of that feeling that "the curtain had blown aside for a moment", revealing a glimpse of another dimension.

Where we all live in East Sussex, deer (usually fallow, not roe) are increasingly present, often dangerously so on dark roads. But however often we see them, and however much we deplore the damage they do to our farms and our gardens, every sighting still catches us up short. We cannot fail to respond to the mystery of their "secret deerhood".

On a Night of Snow

BY ELIZABETH COATSWORTH 1893–1986

Cat, if you go outdoors, you must walk in the snow.
You will come back with little white shoes on your feet,
little white shoes of snow that have heels of sleet.
Stay by the fire, my Cat. Lie still, do not go.
See how the flames are leaping and hissing low.
I will bring you a saucer of milk like a marguerite,
so white and so smooth, so spherical and so sweet –
stay with me, Cat. Outdoors the wild winds blow.

Outdoors the wild winds blow, Mistress, and dark is the
   night,
strange voices cry in the trees, intoning strange lore,
and more than cats move, lit by our eyes' green light,
on silent feet where the meadow grasses hang hoar –
Mistress, there are portents abroad of magic and might,
and things that are yet to be done. Open the door!

Inside, outside. Warm, cold. Light, dark. Cautious, daring. Tame, wild. This little poem pulls us both ways. We
discussed which of us would choose to stay by the fire

and which would seek out the "things that are yet to be done", with one of the two Carolines in each camp. "Once I'd have been in the latter category, but perhaps not now," said 95-year-old Pam.

The hinge of the poem – the repetition of "outdoors the wild winds blow" – is a brilliant way of demonstrating how fear and danger seen in a mirror become thrill and mystery. The double use of feet is clever, too; the charming "little white shoes of snow that have heels of sleet" in the first part – Sarah N found these particularly appealing – then the invisible, magical "silent feet" of the second. The mistress needs the cat if she is to feel safe, but we all agreed when Caroline T declared that she would lose this argument, and the cat's "Open the door!" would be obeyed.

Romance

BY W.J. TURNER 1889–1946

When I was but thirteen or so
I went into a golden land,
Chimborazo, Cotopaxi
Took me by the hand.

My father died, my brother too,
They passed like fleeting dreams,
I stood where Popocatapetl
In the sunlight gleams.

I dimly heard the master's voice
And boys far off at play, –
Chimborazo, Cotopaxi
Had stolen me away.

I walked in a great golden dream
To and fro from school –
Shining Popocatapetl
The dusty streets did rule.

I walked home with a gold dark boy
And never a word I'd say,
Chimborazo, Cotopaxi
Had taken my speech away.

I gazed entranced upon his face
Fairer than any flower –
O shining Popocatapetl
It was thy magic hour:

The houses, people, traffic seemed
Thin fading dreams by day;
Chimborazo, Cotopaxi,
They had stolen my soul away!

I first encountered this when my brother Charles was at prep school and he wrote it out in an exercise book, perhaps for handwriting practice. I fell under its spell immediately, which is what must happen if one is to tolerate a poem like this at all. I think it's a poem about becoming a poet. The power of words takes hold of the speaker and draws him away from his old life. Chimborazo, Cotopaxi, Popocatapetl – their incantatory names take possession of him as surely as Stevie Smith's "little creature" (see page 133) or Christina Rossetti's goblins. The magic transforms his perception of the world, as when he looks at the "gold dark boy"; poetry and early adolescent eroticism fuse in a "magic hour".

Chimborazo, Cotopaxi and Popocatapetl are volcanoes, two in Ecuador, one in Mexico. Pam remembered being in Ecuador and seeing the shining, snowy peak of Chimborazo and feeling entranced that she was being transported into the world of the suddenly-remembered poem.

W.J. Turner was Australian, but was living in London when he wrote "Romance". He and Siegfried Sassoon were great friends, in fact housemates at one time, until they quarrelled irrecoverably. Yeats admired his work.

The Ghost's Song

ANON., UNDATED

Wae's me! Wae's me!
The acorn's not yet
Fallen from the tree
That's to grow the wood,
That's to make the cradle,
That's to rock the bairn,
That's to grow a man,
That's to lay me.

"Poor ghost!" said Pepe.

When I was a child, this poem gave me the authentic "time immemorial" shiver. In fact, it still does.

6

TRAVELLERS & WANDERERS

All poets are travellers, even if they never leave their own homes. They wander into the shadowy places of the imagination, then show us how to follow them. Proper names, whether of people or of places, are often particularly important in transporting us, from the exotic lure of "Ozymandias" to the more graspable excitement of Elizabeth Barrett Browning's "Some one said, 'Marseilles!'"

Rigorists

BY MARIANNE MOORE 1887–1972

   "We saw reindeer
browsing," a friend who'd been in Lapland, said:
"finding their own food; they are adapted

   to scant *reino*
or pasture, yet they can run eleven
miles in fifty minutes; the feet spread when

   the snow is soft,
and act as snowshoes. They are rigorists,
however handsomely cutwork artists

   of Lapland and
Siberia elaborate the trace
or saddle girth with sawtooth leather lace.

   One looked at us
with its firm face part brown, part white – a queen
of alpine flowers. Santa Claus' reindeer, seen

   at last, had grey-
brown fur, with a neck like edelweiss or
lion's foot – *leontopodium* more

exactly." And
this candelabrum-headed ornament
for a place where ornaments are scarce, sent

to Alaska,
was a gift preventing the extinction
of the Eskimo. The battle was won

by a quiet man,
Sheldon Jackson, evangel to that race
whose reprieve he read in the reindeer's face.

"I can see no reason for calling my work poetry except that there is no other category in which to put it," said Marianne Moore. Perhaps the word "work" is the key; her close observations, showcased by intricate syntax and precise vocabulary, create a "worked" beauty like scrimshaw or filigree. The reindeer are "rigorists", and so is Moore; strictly controlled, unindulgent. Michael W commented on how the prose-like sentences are cut up and spread out, like paper snipped up by scissors, to call attention to the words and details Moore wants us to notice most.

Sheldon Jackson was a Presbyterian missionary of

the later 19th century who devoted much of his life to saving the native peoples of the Alaska Territory. Most people would now censure his attempts to suppress their languages, but he did so because he believed that Americanisation was the key to survival. He saved thousands of artefacts, most now housed in the museum in Sitka that bears his name. Worried by the decline in whale and seal populations, Jackson imported 1,300 reindeer from Siberia to bolster the livelihoods of the Alaskan Eskimos. For this he wins Marianne Moore's admiring respect, though it might be only a "reprieve" he's gained for them.

Ozymandias

BY PERCY BYSSHE SHELLEY 1792–1822

I met a traveller from an antique land
Who said: Two vast and trunkless legs of stone
Stand in the desert. Near them, on the sand,
Half sunk, a shattered visage lies, whose frown,
And wrinkled lip, and sneer of cold command,
Tell that its sculptor well those passions read
Which yet survive, stamped on these lifeless things,
The hand that mocked them, and the heart that fed;
And on the pedestal these words appear:
"My name is Ozymandias, king of kings:
Look on my works, ye Mighty, and despair!"
Nothing besides remains. Round the decay
Of that colossal wreck, boundless and bare
The lone and level sands stretch far away.

and Ozymandias

BY HORACE SMITH 1779–1849

In Egypt's sandy silence, all alone,
Stands a gigantic Leg, which far off throws
The only shadow that the Desert knows:—
"I am great OZYMANDIAS," saith the stone,
"The King of Kings; this mighty City shows
The wonders of my hand." – The City's gone, –
Naught but the Leg remaining to disclose
The site of this forgotten Babylon.
We wonder, – and some Hunter may express
Wonder like ours, when thro' the wilderness
Where London stood, holding the Wolf in chace,
He meets some fragment huge, and stops to guess
What powerful but unrecorded race
Once dwelt in that annihilated place.

These two young poetical friends decided to compete
with each other in writing a sonnet about the broken
statue of the Egyptian pharaoh Rameses II who reigned
in the 13th century BC, and created a city in the desert.
(His triumphs are recorded on the so-called Cleopatra's

Needle.) They used his Greek name, Ozymandias, because their source was the Greek historian Diodorus Siculus who had described the massive statue and quoted the inscription on its base: "King of Kings Ozymandias am I. If any want to know how great I am and where I lie, let him outdo me in my work." Neither Shelley nor Smith had been to Egypt, but since Napoleon's 1798–1801 Egyptian campaign, interest in and knowledge of the ancient civilisation had hugely increased, and artefacts made their way to Europe. The British Museum had announced the acquisition of a large fragment of a statue to be transported from Thebes, and the sonneteers knew about this, though they hadn't seen it; it didn't arrive in London until 1821.

The competition was a friendly one, and it is easy to see who won. Shelley's sonnet has become one of the most recited and anthologised poems in the English canon; Smith's hasn't. Part of Shelley's success is that he exactly captures that scalp-prickling shiver that everyone feels when they contemplate the ruins of the ancient past. How wise he is to exclude all names except the towering polysyllabic "Ozymandias", magnificently exotic with its "zy", but still pronounceable. His anonymous "traveller from an antique land" is Diodorus, whom he "met" on paper, so here's an aside about time-travelling through the miraculous power of literature. From the second line, it's the traveller speaking. Shelley is merely the conduit. This is brilliant; we absorb the traveller's words undiluted by any secondary conclusion-drawing or moral-pointing. There is, of course, a moral – a very strong one – but we don't just read it, we *feel* it.

Shelley hated tyranny and oppression. The power of this tyrant has fallen away, destroyed by the sands of the desert and by the sands of time. The sculptor, employed to immortalise the greatness of the King of Kings, left us his "sneer of cold command" which is his essence, outliving all other attributes. The most important word in the poem is "nothing". Shelley was an atheist. He leaves us with an image of the minuteness and futility of human achievement in an empty infinity – "the lone and level sands stretch far away". How perfect to end on that open vowel sound, that long, long "a". Everyone thought this was superb, because people will if they like poetry at all.

On to Horace Smith. We had fun with this one. Not a bad first line, but then, oh dear, that Leg. The capital makes it even worse. "It's Monty Python!" said Michael W. Things improve in the sestet, which is actually pretty good. While Percy concentrated on the hubris of the tyrant, Horace asks us to imagine specifically our own downfall, the end of civilisation as we know it – "the wilderness where London stood". It's interesting that Smith envisages wilding, including the return of wolves, once native to Britain but long extinct by 1818. It's salutary to think of ourselves as "unrecorded", and of London, by Smith's day the mightiest city in the world, as "annihilated".

Henrietta, a poet herself, wondered whether Smith saw Shelley's effort before his own was published (they both appeared in Leigh Hunt's "Examiner", but in different issues) and thought that if he did, he would have felt rather sheepish. When Smith's poem was republished years later, he added an extended title: "On a stupendous Leg of granite, Discovered standing by Itself in the Deserts of Egypt, with the Inscription Inserted Below". We all agreed this didn't help at all.

from **Aurora Leigh Book VII**

BY ELIZABETH BARRETT BROWNING 1806–1861

        I just knew it when we swept
Above the old roofs of Dijon: Lyons dropped
A spark into the night, half trodden out
Unseen. But presently the winding Rhone
Washed out the moonlight large along his banks
Which strained their yielding curves out clear and clean
To hold it, – shadow of town and castle blurred
Upon the hurrying river. Such an air
Blew thence upon the forehead, – half an air
And half a water, – that I leaned and looked,
Then, turning back on Marian, smiled to mark
That she looked only on her child, who slept,
His face toward the moon too.

So we passed
The liberal open country and the close,
And shot through tunnels, like a lightning-wedge
By great Thor-hammers driven through the rock,
Which, quivering through the intestine blackness, splits,
And lets it in at once: the train swept in
Athrob with effort, trembling with resolve,
The fierce denouncing whistle wailing on
And dying off smothered in the shuddering dark,
While we, self-awed, drew troubled breath, oppressed

As other Titans underneath the pile
And nightmare of the mountains. Out, at last,
To catch the dawn afloat upon the land!
– Hills, slung forth broadly and gauntly everywhere,
Not crampt in their foundations, pushing wide
Rich outspreads of the vineyards and the corn,
(As if they entertained i' the name of France)
While, down their straining sides, streamed manifest
A soil as red as Charlemagne's knightly blood,
To consecrate the verdure. Some one said,
"Marseilles!" And lo, the city of Marseilles,
With all her ships behind her, and beyond,
The scimitar of ever-shining sea
For right-hand use, bared blue against the sky!

Aurora Leigh is a "novel poem" of contemporary life in nine books. Aurora is the narrator, a young, single, well-educated orphan who strikes out independently to try to achieve greatness – and a living wage – through writing poetry. In this section, she is travelling by steam train across Europe in the company of the ironically named Marian Erle, a self-taught working-class girl whose drunken mother tried to sell her into prostitution. Marian has a baby son, the result of rape. Aurora offers

Marian a marriage "of sorts"; why should they not do without men, and travel together to Italy with the child in search of a new life?

"Victorian Interrailing!" exclaimed Caroline F with glee, and indeed this passage captures the thrill of a journey into the unknown; doubly thrilling in 1856, when a long train journey was still a novelty, and travelling without male chaperones almost unheard of. Aurora has a poet's response to everything she sees; everything is animate. Marian is wholly absorbed in creation of another kind; she cannot take her eyes off her sleeping child.

Sue was pleasantly surprised by the toughness and originality of the language. David liked the exotic promise of the "scimitar of ever-shining sea... bared blue against the sky". Elizabeth Barrett Browning herself said that this very long poem was "the one into which my highest convictions about Life and Art have entered".

Sonnet: In Orknay

BY WILLIAM FOWLER C.1560–1612

Upon the utmost corners of the warld,
and on the borders of this massive round,
quhaire fates and fortoune hither hes me harld,
I doe deplore my greiffs upon this ground;
and seing roring seis from roks rebound
by ebbs and streames of contrair routing tyds,
and phebus chariot in there wawes ly dround,
quha equallye now night and day devyds,
I cal to mynde the storms my thoughts abyds,
which euer wax and never dois decress,
for nights of dole dayes Ioys ay ever hyds,
and in there vayle doith al my weill suppress:
so this I see, quhaire ever I remove,
I chainge bot sees, but can not chainge my love.

St Andrews-educated William Fowler, as well as being a
"makar" (a bard to the royal court) was a spy, recruited
by Elizabeth I's spymaster Francis Walsingham. He was
part of the circle of James VI of Scotland (later James I
of England), taught the king "the art of memory", and
became Master of Requests to James' consort Anne of

Denmark. He was well-travelled, visiting Paris, London, Denmark and Norway as well as the far-flung and apparently disagreeable "Orknay". "The sophistication of the sonnet form comes up against the primitive remoteness of Orkney, and that's where the energy comes from," said Michael W. We all agreed that the 16th-century Scottish spelling added to the turbulence and muscularity of this rather thrilling sonnet, but in the interests of clarity, here is my modernised version.

> Upon the utmost corners of the world,
> and on the borders of this massive round,
> where fates and fortune hither have me hurled,
> I do deplore my griefs upon this ground;
> and seeing roaring seas from rocks rebound
> by ebbs and streams of counter-flowing tides,
> and Phoebus' chariot in their waves lies drowned
> which equally now night and day divides
> I call to mind the storms my thoughts abide,
> which ever grow and never do decrease,
> for nights of sorrow day's joys always hide
> and in their shade do all my weal suppress.
> So this I see, that wherever I move,
> I can change seas, but cannot change my love.

Phoebus' chariot is the sun. Fowler was the uncle of William Drummond of Hawthornden, whose "Phoebus, Arise" I have included in Chapter 7.

Lost Love

BY ROBERT GRAVES 1895–1985

His eyes are quickened so with grief,
He can watch a grass or leaf
Every instant grow; he can
Clearly through a flint wall see,
Or watch the startled spirit flee
From the throat of a dead man.
Across two counties he can hear
And catch your words before you speak.
The woodlouse or the maggot's weak
Clamour rings in his sad ear,
And noise so slight it would surpass
Credence – drinking sound of grass,
Worm talk, clashing jaws of moth
Chumbling holes in cloth;
The groan of ants who undertake
Gigantic loads for honour's sake
Whir of spiders when they spin,
And minute whispering, mumbling, sighs
Of idle grubs and flies.
This man is quickened so with grief,
He wanders god-like or like thief
Inside and out, below, above,
Without relief seeking lost love.

Graves, who had been almost fatally wounded at the Battle of the Somme, wrote this when he was 24 and recently demobilised. He had suffered from shellshock; the heightened, tortured sensibilities described in the poem seem to relate to that. In his war memoir *Good-bye To All That* he described his fragility: "Since 1916, the fear of gas obsessed me. Any unusual smell, even a sudden strong scent of flowers in a garden, was enough to send me trembling. And I couldn't face the sound of heavy shelling now; the noise of a car back-firing would send me flat on my face, or running for cover."

Graves' early romantic attachments were mainly for other men, though after the war his life was dominated by passionate relationships with women. In "Lost Love" he is careful not to identify the wanderer's love object, and though he may be thinking of a dead fellow soldier, the group felt that the title should not be interpreted too literally. "He's mourning for the world he's lost," said Michael W. "It's not a love poem, it's a war poem," said Shelagh.

He Looked At Me

BY A.E. HOUSMAN 1859–1936

He looked at me with eyes I thought
I was not like to find,
The voice he begged for pence with brought
Another man to mind.

Oh no, lad, never touch your cap;
It is not my half-crown;
You have it from a better chap
That long ago lay down.

Turn east and over Thames to Kent
And come to the sea's brim,
And find his everlasting tent
And touch your cap to him.

As a young man in the 1880s, A.E. Housman shared
London lodgings with two brothers, Moses and Adalbert
Jackson. Both meant a great deal to him. Moses was the
unrequited love of his life; it may have been an unwel-
comed declaration of this love that caused Housman to

move out into separate accommodation. He also had a *tendresse* for Adalbert, who went to India and died there only a few years later. In this poem, published in 1936, Housman meets a young man begging on a London street and is pierced with the memory of Adalbert. The half-crown he gives the beggar is a memorial to his lost friend, but it also feels as if he's passing on a token of homosexual acknowledgement, a kind of Masonic handshake.

A strange benefit of reading poetry is that it pulls you into the orbit of temperaments very different to your own. By nature I am nothing like pessimistic, introverted, misogynistic Housman, but my appetite for the gloom and pathos of his poems knows (almost) no bounds.

The Embankment

BY T.E. HULME 1883–1917

(The fantasia of a fallen gentleman on a cold, bitter night)

Once, in finesse of fiddles found I ecstasy,
In the flash of gold heels on the hard pavement.
Now see I
That warmth's the very stuff of poesy.
Oh, God, make small
The old star-eaten blanket of the sky,
That I may fold it round me and in comfort lie.

T.E. Hulme was twice sent down from Cambridge, once for rowdy behaviour, once for "a scandal involving a Roedean girl". These details suggest that he felt affinity with his "fallen gentleman". Sarah N loved the delicate precision of the choice of words, and the idea of stars nibbling the "blanket of the sky" like moths.

Hulme's poetic output was tiny – 25 poems – but his influence was great. He is credited with having written the first Imagist poem ("Autumn"). He joined the artillery and was killed by a shell in Flanders, aged 34; he was apparently too deep in thought to get out of its way.

7

SUN, MOON, STARS & PLANETS

Poets pull poems out of the sky – Keats describes this process in his sonnet "When I Have Fears That I May Cease to Be":

> When I behold, upon the night's starred face,
> Huge cloudy symbols of a high romance,
> And think that I may never live to trace
> Their shadows, with the magic hand of chance...

Human fascination with the sun, moon and stars has translated itself into poetry since literacy began, as seen in the Anglo-Saxon riddle I've included in this section.

Phoebus, Arise

BY WILLIAM DRUMMOND OF HAWTHORNDEN 1585–1649

Phoebus, arise,
And paint the sable skies
With azure, white, and red;
Rouse Memnon's mother from her Tithon's bed
That she thy career may with roses spread;
The nightingales thy coming each where sing;
Make an eternal spring;
Give life to this dark world which lieth dead.
Spread forth thy golden hair
In larger locks than thou wast wont before,
And emperor-like, decore
With diadem of pearl thy temples fair.
Chase hence the ugly night,
Which serves but to make dear thy glorious light.
This is that happy morn,
That day, long wished day
Of all my life so dark,
(If cruel stars have not my ruin sworn,
And fates not hope betray)
Which, only white, deserves
A diamond forever it should mark:
This is the morn should bring unto this grove
My love, to hear and recompense my love.

Fair king, who all preserves,
But show thy blushing beams,
And thou two sweeter eyes
Shalt see than those which by Peneus' streams
Did once thy heart surprise;
Nay, suns, which shine as clear
As thou when two thou did to Rome appear,
Now Flora, deck thyself in fairest guise;
If that ye, winds, would hear
A voice surpassing far Amphion's lyre,
Your stormy chiding stay;
Let Zephyr only breathe
And with her tresses play,
Kissing sometimes these purple ports of death.
The winds all silent are,
And Phoebus in his chair,
Ensaffroning sea and air,
Makes vanish every star;
Night like a drunkard reels
Beyond the hills to shun his flaming wheels;
The fields with flow'rs are decked in every hue,
The clouds bespangle with bright gold their blue;
Here is the pleasant place,
And ev'ry thing save her, who all should grace.

William Drummond was Scottish – indeed, he was the laird of Hawthornden, in Midlothian; his castle is now a writers' retreat. His courtly poetry, however, has no Scotch flavour. In this sumptuous yet anxious poem, he orders Phoebus, god of the sun, to prepare the landscape as a suitably gorgeous setting for the declaration of his love; colours, roses, nightingales, jewels, and above all, light, to transform his "life so dark". We wait with the speaker for the arrival of his beloved, whose beauties and graces outshine everything recorded in classical poetry. It's tense. "The winds all silent are." Phoebus paints the universe gold – what a marvellous word "ensaffroning" is, holding as it does scent and taste as well as colour. Ugly night has reeled drunkenly into hiding. Everything is ready. But where is She?

Opinion in the group was divided as to whether she really had stood him up. Caroline F, always optimistic, thought that she'd just been a little delayed. Olivia feared the worst – Drummond has sown the seeds of worry earlier in the poem. We all puzzled over "purple ports of death"; Amanda found out that they were the lips of the beloved, and that kissing them would cause the kisser to die of ecstasy. (Perhaps it's just as well if she doesn't show up.) "I've heard of purple prose," said Caroline "but this is purple poetry."

Blazing in Gold and Quenching in Purple

BY EMILY DICKINSON 1830–1886

Blazing in Gold and quenching in Purple
Leaping like Leopards to the Sky
Then at the feet of the old Horizon
Laying her spotted Face to die
Stooping as low as the Otter's Window
Touching the Roof and tinting the Barn
Kissing her Bonnet to the Meadow
And the Juggler of Day is gone.

A brilliant burst of Emily energy. "Look at all those exuberant 'ing' endings," said Olivia. The whole group loved the fact that this sun is female.

Some versions have "oriel" window or "kitchen" window, but of course we all preferred "otter's" window. How could you not?

Riddle of Moon and Sun (Anglo-Saxon)

EXETER BOOK NUMBER 28, LATE 10TH CENTURY

Ic wiht geseah   wundorlice
hornum bitweonum   huthe laedan,
lyftfaet leohtlic   listum gegierwed,
huthe to tham hame   of tham heresithe;
walde hyre on thaere byrig   bur atimbran,
searwum asettan,   gif hit swa meahte.
Tha cwom wundorlicu wiht   ofer wealles hrof,
seo is eallum cuth   eorthbuendum;
ahredde tha tha huthe,   and to ham bedraf
wreccan ofer willan,   gewat hyre west thonan
faehthum feran,   forth onette.
Dust stonc to heofonum,   deaw feol on eorthan,
niht forth gewat.   Naenig siththan
wera gewiste   thaere wihte sith.

MY VERSION

I saw a being, wondrous,
Plunder hoarded between its horns,
Bright shining cup of air
Creeping home with spoils of war
Seeking where to build
A secret treasure-house.
Then over the house-walls
A stranger creature rose –
Strange, yet known by all
Who dwell here on the earth;
He grabbed the loot, drove the pale wretch
Home against his will;
Then westwards rolled the hostile one.
Dust rose to heaven, dew fell to earth,
Night followed, sure. But where that creature went –
No man on earth knows that.

Anglo-Saxon, or Old English, is inscrutable to the general reader in a way that Middle English – the English of Chaucer – isn't. It's not just the vocabulary and grammar that are mysterious; what remains of

Anglo-Saxon poetry (and who knows how much has been lost?) reveals an unfamiliar way of looking at the world, a different set of poetic priorities. Love, for instance, barely features as a subject. Indeed, joy of any kind is in short supply. Fighting and bewailing predominate, along with a fascination with enigma.

Riddles like this one seem to have been popular with our pre-Conquest forbears. These riddles are not jokes. They are mental puzzles; they aim to make you consider familiar things from an oblique angle, and, in the process, perhaps ponder essential truths.

Anglo-Saxon verse never rhymes; it's held together by alliteration, and a fairly regular nine- or ten-syllable line with a break in the middle of each. The result is incantatory.

If you alliterate a lot, you need to be ingenious in finding synonyms. Anglo-Saxon uses a lot of compound nouns and adjectives; here, for example, "lyftfaet" (literally, air vessel) and "eorthbuendum" (earth-inhabitants). The poetry-makers were often, in effect, coining new words. This adds to the obscurity and to the fascination.

I made my own version of the Riddle of the Moon and Sun. This isn't a scholarly translation, more an attempt at explanation. What struck me was how free the little poem was from our received ideas of how to portray the sun and moon. These are not objects of beauty, symbols of love, of passion, of death or rebirth, nor are they godlike. They are odd unadmirable creatures, the moon a furtive thief, the sun a violent thug. And, in the 10th century, once they were out of sight, no one knew where they'd gone.

"I think it's significant that some of our greatest recent poets such as Ted Hughes and Seamus Heaney have relished and translated Anglo-Saxon verse," said Michael W. Caroline T recalled her primary school days, when "my teachers taught me that we know almost nothing about the thinking of the Anglo-Saxons. This left a lingering mystery and frustration. So when we read the poem, my old longing to have some insight into the minds of those ancient peoples was suddenly fulfilled."

"The reading in Anglo-Saxon with the sounds of the fire crackling seemed fabulous," said Veronica. "You don't need to understand it to experience the atmosphere – a little bastion against the world strengthened by the group."

Full Moon

BY ALICE OSWALD 1966–

Good God!
What did I dream last night?
I dreamt I was the moon.
I woke and found myself still asleep.

It was like this: my face misted up from inside
And I came and went at will through a little peephole.
I had no voice, no mouth, nothing to express my trouble,
except my shadows leaning downhill, not quite parallel.

Something needs to be said to describe my moonlight.
Almost frost but softer, almost ash but wholer.
Made almost of water, which has strictly speaking
No feature, but a kind of counter-light, call it insight.

Like in woods, when they jostle their hooded shapes,
Their heads congealed together, having murdered each
    other,
There are moon-beings, sound-beings, such as deer and
    half-deer
Passing through there, whose eyes can pierce through
    things.
I was like that: visible invisible visible invisible.
There's no material as variable as moonlight.

I was climbing, clinging to the underneath of my bones,
    thinking:
Good God! Who have I been last night?

Here Alice Oswald channels some of that Anglo-Saxon weirdery. "Almost frost but softer, almost ash but wholer" – that could come straight from an Old English riddle. Deer and half-deer, shapes you can just glimpse out of the corner of your mind's eye. And that question at the end; the authentic prickle at the back of the neck.

"She's turned herself inside out," said Olivia. David thought the poem was like a photographic negative. Everyone agreed that Oswald has captured the eerie, transformative connection we feel with the full moon.

On the Eclipse of the Moon, October 1865

BY CHARLES TENNYSON TURNER 1808–1879

One little noise of life remain'd – I heard
The train pause in the distance, then rush by,
Brawling and hushing, like some busy fly
That murmurs and then settles; nothing stirr'd
Beside. The shadow of our travelling earth
Hung on the silver moon, which mutely went
Through that grand process, without token sent,
Or any sign to call a gazer forth,
Had I not chanced to see; dumb was the vault
Of heaven, and dumb the fields – no zephyr swept
The forest walks, or through the coppice crept;
Nor other sound the stillness did assault,
Save that faint-brawling railway's move and halt;
So perfect was the silence Nature kept.

Older brother of the more famous Alfred, Charles Tennyson Turner (he annexed the extra surname after a legacy
from an uncle) was an Anglican clergyman who turned
out sonnets with a dab hand, like neat little word-pies.

Here, the busyness and littleness of the steam train, a proud and relatively recent invention of Man, makes the "grand process" of Nature seem all the more mysterious and magnificent. "The shadow of our travelling earth/ Hung on the silver moon" is beautiful; how dignified that kind of travelling is, compared to the "faint-brawling" railway. It's hard to write a poem about Man's insignificance without sounding melancholy or despairing, but CTT manages it here.

The Unending Sky

BY JOHN MASEFIELD 1878–1967

I could not sleep for thinking of the sky,
The unending sky, with all its million suns
Which turn their planets everlastingly
In nothing, where the fire-haired comet runs.
If I could sail that nothing, I should cross
Silence and emptiness with dark stars passing,
Then, in the darkness, see a point of gloss
Burn to a glow, and glare, and keep amassing,
And rage into a sun with wandering planets
And drop behind, and then, as I proceed,
See his last light upon his last moon's granites
Die to dark that would be night indeed.
Night where my soul might sail a million years
In nothing, not even death, not even tears.

This is the twelfth poem in Masefield's Lollingdon
Downs cycle. It could be seen as an oblique response
to the nihilistic ravages of the Great War, seen at first
hand by Masefield who, though old enough to be exempt
from military service, worked as an orderly in a frontline
hospital.

Everyone associates Masefield with sailing ("I must down to the seas again"), but here he sails not on water but in, or on, or through, nothing. This is a rather magnificent attempt to explore what nothing is.

Bright Star

BY JOHN KEATS 1795–1821

Bright star, would I were steadfast as thou art –
Not in lone splendour hung aloft the night
And watching, with eternal lids apart,
Like nature's patient, sleepless eremite,
The moving waters at their priestlike task
Of pure ablution round earth's human shores,
Or gazing on the new soft-fallen mask
Of snow upon the mountains and the moors –
No – yet still steadfast, still unchangeable,
Pillow'd upon my fair love's ripening breast,
To feel for ever its soft fall and swell,
Awake for ever in a sweet unrest,
Still, still to hear her tender-taken breath,
And so live ever – or else swoon to death.

and At Lulworth Cove a Century Back

BY THOMAS HARDY, 1840–1928

Had I but lived a hundred years ago
I might have gone, as I have gone this year,
By Warmwell Cross on to a Cove I know,
And Time have placed his finger on me there:

"*You see that man?*" – I might have looked, and said,
"O yes: I see him. One that boat has brought
Which dropped down Channel round Saint Alban's
   Head.
So commonplace a youth calls not my thought."

"*You see that man?*" – "Why yes; I told you; yes:
Of an idling town-sort; thin; hair brown in hue;
And as the evening light scants less and less
He looks up at a star, as many do."

"*You see that man?*" – "Nay, leave me!" then I plead,
"I have fifteen miles to vamp across the lea,
And it grows dark, and I am weary-kneed:
I have said the third time; yes, that man I see!"

"Good. That man goes to Rome – to death, despair;
And no one notes him now but you and I:

A hundred years, and the world will follow him there,
And bend with reverence where his ashes lie."

Fellow poets and readers alike quickly adapted the facts to shape their own version of the story of Keats' short life and agonising decline and death. Shelley started the process with his "Adonais"; the divinely gifted young man, "neglected and apart", slain by the cruel arrows of unfeeling critics. Byron's take was more cynical – "'Tis strange the mind, that very fiery particle,/Should let itself be snuffed out by an article." Neither version does justice to Keats' ambition, pugnacity and sensuality.

Keats' own friends – there were many, and they loved him – tended to embellish little stories to emphasise his importance in their lives, and theirs in his. The artist Joseph Severn, who accompanied Keats on the journey to Rome that was a desperate and doomed attempt to cure him of consumption, and who nursed him on his long-drawn-out deathbed, created a pleasing legend about the "Bright Star" sonnet. In September 1820, the ship taking Keats and Severn to Italy, held up by bad weather, made an unscheduled stop on the Dorset coast. Scrambling among the "splendid caverns and grottos" of Lulworth Cove, Keats seemed "like his former self";

back on board he scribbled down the sonnet, then asked Severn to copy it on "a blank leaf in a folio volume of Shakespeare's *Poems*". For nearly ever after, people believed that this was how and when "Bright Star" was written. It is often proclaimed as "His Last Poem" in older editions of collected Keats.

Hardy certainly believed this version. It suited his purposes perfectly. Exactly a century later, he wrote this musing tribute. He imagines himself at Lulworth in 1820; Time, personified, insistently points out Keats, looking up at a star; this apparently "commonplace" young man will achieve literary immortality. "It's not really about Keats," said Michael W. "It's what Hardy wants for himself." Like Keats, Hardy was of humble origin, not rich, savaged by critics. The idea that Keats the Londoner found the inspiration for his most transcendently beautiful poem at Lulworth, in Hardy's own territory (scene of Sergeant Troy's sexy Channel swim in *Far From the Madding Crowd*), was too marvellous to be scrutinised for historical accuracy. Time places his finger on Hardy for a clear reason – Hardy, too, will one day have worshippers who "bend in reverence".

We still can't be sure when "Bright Star" was written, but we do know it predates September 1820. I'll throw in my lot with Keats' biographer Andrew Motion, who says October 1819, just before Keats' 24th birthday. What I do feel sure of is that it is about Fanny Brawne, with whom Keats was passionately and obsessively in love. His feelings about the women who had previously attracted him fade into the common light of day in comparison with his (more or less requited) love for Fanny. This is her "ripening breast" all right.

Fanny is not the "bright star". That, surely, is Arcturus, the North Star. Keats contemplates its remote beauty as it gazes down, keeping uncomplaining watch over a world imbued with natural, cleansing holiness – "the moving waters at their priestlike task/Of pure ablution round earth's human shores". The "urus" part of Arcturus means "guardian" in Greek; the star is a benef- icent guardian of the world which has the lovers at its centre. The fall of snow softening the contours of the landscape, a parallel, perhaps, to sheets draping the contours of the sleeping girl, was a view only available in those pre-flight days to a few intrepid balloonists, or to the imagination of a poet. Keats doesn't want the star's "lone splendour"; he wants its steadfastness, its immortal- ity. In one great swooping sentence he moves from outer space through the earth's atmosphere, over sea and land and into the warm place where his beloved lies, where life achieves its most exquisite and intense expression. If only he had the star's steadfastness, he could live in this state of bliss for ever. If he can't have this, he'd rather "swoon to death".

Keats always speaks to us through our senses. In "Bright Star" he starts by looking, and ends by touching and listening in the dark. "Those delicate 't' sounds in 'tender-taken' make you really feel it, somehow," said Sarah F. The movement from detached admiration to deep intimacy is framed by negatives – "Not... No" – the most positive negatives in poetry.

Now the Hungry Lion Roars

BY WILLIAM SHAKESPEARE 1564–1616
from A MIDSUMMER-NIGHT'S DREAM

Now the hungry lion roars,
And the wolf behowls the moon;
Whilst the heavy ploughman snores,
All with weary task fordone.
Now the wasted brands do glow,
Whilst the screech-owl, screeching loud,
Puts the wretch that lies in woe
In remembrance of a shroud.
Now it is the time of night,
That the graves, all gaping wide,
Every one lets forth his sprite,
In the churchway paths to glide:
And we fairies, that do run
By the triple Hecate's team,
From the presence of the sun,
Following darkness like a dream,
Now are frolic; not a mouse
Shall disturb this hallowed house:
I am sent with broom before
To sweep the dust behind the door.

This is one of Puck's songs; it leaves us unsure whether he is a "merry wanderer of the night", as he describes himself, or something more sinister, a "shrewd and knavish sprite". I've always relished the feeling that things happen in a house at night, unseen, and I love this mixture of the supernatural and the domestic. The last two lines seem full of a significance that whisks just out of sight like a mouse's tail.

Our local Sussex poet, Rudyard Kipling, made plenty of use of Puck three centuries later. Mike F works at Bateman's, Kipling's house, where a suitably ambivalent statue of Puck, gleeful and a little sinister, greets visitors.

8

JOY & SORROW

The poems I've chosen for this section span 700 years, demonstrating that our modes of expression may change but our core emotions stay the same. One of the most consistently important functions of poetry has been to shape these emotions and help us to recognise them and manage them.

The Bridal Morn

ANON., C.1500

The maidens came
When I was in my mother's bower;
I had all that I would.
The bailey beareth the bell away
The lily, the rose, the rose I lay.

The silver is white, red is the gold;
The robes they lay in fold.
The bailey beareth the bell away;
The lily, the rose, the rose I lay.

And through the glass window shines the sun.
How should I love, and I so young?
The bailey beareth the bell away;
The lily, the rose, the rose I lay.

This is one of my desert island poems. Every word is perfect.

Like many lyrics of its period, its origins are obscure, as is some of its meaning. This is what I think about it. I see a young girl, rich, desirable both for herself and as a commodity in the marriage market, at the exact moment of transition from child to woman. Her bridesmaids prepare her for this transition; she leaves the cocoon of her "mother's bower" for dazzling exposure to the world and the future – "and through the glass window shines the sun". Is she standing in church at this moment, taking her marriage vows? This is how Shelagh envisaged it. Or does the "glass window" (glass was a sign of affluence) belong to the grand dwelling she has left, or the one she has just entered as a bride?

The wedding bell echoes round the castle tower; like the sound, she is borne away, from the old life to the new. She has all the worldly goods she could desire – the silver, the gold, the robes that "lay in fold", encapsulating all the promise and potential of her future. It is thrilling, but there is anxiety too. "The lily, the rose, the rose I lay"– one moment she's pale as a lily, the next blushing like a rose. The flowers also suggest the change she is undergoing, the lily symbolising virginal purity, the rose blooming womanhood.

The bridegroom is conspicuous by his absence. The girl is not thinking about him, but about her own state of mind, at this most crucial moment of her life. "How should I love, and I so young?" How, indeed? I can think of no poem where the painful joy of entering the adult world is more acutely expressed.

"It's so beautiful and evocative, it makes me feel a bit tearful," said Polly. "It's as if the poem itself is the glass window and we're looking through it," said Pam.

What Wild Dawns There Were

BY DENISE LEVERTOV 1923–1997

What wild dawns there were
   in our first years here
when we would run outdoors naked
to pee in the long grass behind the house
   and see over the hills such streamers,
   such banners full of fire and blue (the blue
   that is Lilith to full day's honest Eve) –
What feathers of gold under the morning star
   we saw from dazed eyes before
stumbling back to bed chilled with dew
to sleep till the sun was high!

Now if we wake early
   we don't go outdoors – or I don't –
   and you if you do go
   rarely call me to see the day break.
I watch the dawn through glass: this year
   only cloudless flushes of light, paleness
   slowly turning to rose,
   and fading subdued.
We have not spoken of these tired
risings of the sun.

"This marriage is over!" said Caroline F. The breakdown is expressed in the choppy second verse; "we don't go outdoors – or I don't –". How well "I watch the dawn through glass" sums up that sad falling-away of passion that the group agreed was the usual, though not absolutely inevitable, experience. We read this in conjunction with John Donne's "The Sunne Rising", that ebullient celebration of the beginning of the process.

We were intrigued by Lilith, who was Adam's first wife in Jewish folklore, and created equal to him; not, as Eve was, from a mere rib. Lilith stood for sexual wantonness, and came to be seen as demonically dangerous. We felt sorry that this interesting figure doesn't feature more prominently in Christian-derived culture. Denise Levertov's Jewish father (her mother was Welsh) became an Anglican minister; he was, she said "steeped in Jewish and Christian scholarship and mysticism". Levertov became an American citizen, based in New York. "What Wild Dawns There Were" feels as if it is set in Maine, where she and her writer husband spent their summers.

The Courtship of the Yonghy-Bonghy-Bo

BY EDWARD LEAR, 1812–1888

On the coast of Coromandel
  Where the early pumpkins blow,
    In the middle of the woods
  Lived the Yonghy-Bonghy-Bo.
Two old chairs, and half a candle,
One old jug without a handle –
    These were all his worldly goods,
    In the middle of the woods,
    These were all the worldly goods,
  Of the Yonghy-Bonghy-Bo,
  Of the Yonghy-Bonghy-Bo.

Once, among the Bong-trees walking
  Where the early pumpkins blow,
    To a little heap of stones
  Came the Yonghy-Bonghy-Bo.
There he heard a Lady talking,
To some milk-white Hens of Dorking –
    " 'Tis the Lady Jingly Jones!
    On that little heap of stones
    Sits the Lady Jingly Jones!"
  Said the Yonghy-Bonghy-Bo,
  Said the Yonghy-Bonghy-Bo.

194

"Lady Jingly! Lady Jingly!
  Sitting where the pumpkins blow,
    Will you come and be my wife?"
  Said the Yonghy-Bonghy-Bo.
"I am tired of living singly —
On this coast so wild and shingly —
    I'm a-weary of my life;
    If you'll come and be my wife,
    Quite serene would be my life!"
  Said the Yonghy-Bonghy-Bo,
  Said the Yonghy-Bonghy-Bo.

"On this Coast of Coromandel
  Shrimps and watercresses grow,
    Prawns are plentiful and cheap,"
  Said the Yonghy-Bonghy-Bo.
"You shall have my chairs and candle,
And my jug without a handle!
    Gaze upon the rolling deep
    (Fish is plentiful and cheap);
    As the sea, my love is deep!"
  Said the Yonghy-Bonghy-Bo,
  Said the Yonghy-Bonghy-Bo.

Lady Jingly answered sadly,
  And her tears began to flow —
    "Your proposal comes too late,
  Mr. Yonghy-Bonghy-Bo!

I would be your wife most gladly!"
(Here she twirled her fingers madly)
   "But in England I've a mate!
   Yes! You've asked me far too late,
   For in England I've a mate,
  Mr. Yonghy-Bonghy-Bo!
  Mr. Yonghy-Bonghy-Bo!

"Mr. Jones (his name is Handel –
  Handel Jones, Esquire, & Co.)
   Dorking fowls delights to send
  Mr. Yonghy-Bonghy-Bo!
Keep, oh, keep your chairs and candle,
And your jug without a handle –
   I can merely be your friend!
   Should my Jones more Dorkings send,
   I will give you three, my friend!
  Mr. Yonghy-Bonghy-Bo!
  Mr. Yonghy-Bonghy-Bo!

"Though you've such a tiny body,
  And your head so large doth grow –
   Though your hat may blow away
  Mr. Yonghy-Bonghy-Bo!
Though you're such a Hoddy Doddy,
Yet I wish that I could modi-
   fy the words I needs must say!
   Will you please to go away?
   That is all I have to say,

Mr. Yonghy-Bonghy-Bo!
Mr. Yonghy-Bonghy-Bo!"

Down the slippery slopes of Myrtle,
  Where the early pumpkins blow,
    To the calm and silent sea
  Fled the Yonghy-Bonghy-Bo.
There, beyond the Bay of Gurtle
Lay a large and lively Turtle.
    "You're the Cove," he said, "for me;
    On your back beyond the sea,
    Turtle, you shall carry me!"
  Said the Yonghy-Bonghy-Bo,
  Said the Yonghy-Bonghy-Bo.

Through the silent-roaring ocean
  Did the Turtle swiftly go;
    Holding fast upon his shell
  Rode the Yonghy-Bonghy-Bo.
With a sad primeval motion
Towards the sunset isles of Boshen
    Still the Turtle bore him well.
    Holding fast upon his shell,
    "Lady Jingly Jones, farewell!"
  Sang the Yonghy-Bonghy-Bo,
  Sang the Yonghy-Bonghy-Bo.

From the coast of Coromandel
  Did that Lady never go;
    On that heap of stones she mourns
  For the Yonghy-Bonghy-Bo.
On that Coast of Coromandel,
In his jug without a handle
    Still she weeps, and daily moans;
    On that little heap of stones
    To her Dorking Hens she moans,
  For the Yonghy-Bonghy-Bo.
  For the Yonghy-Bonghy-Bo.

"I don't know whether to laugh or cry," said Judith. Shelagh was torn between pity for the Yonghy-Bonghy-Bo, and sympathy for Lady Jingly Jones: "'Will you please to go away?' We've all had to say that at some time or other, haven't we?" Lady Jingly's provisional offer of three hens of Dorking to soften the blow is painfully tactless. But in the last verse there's a surprise; her regret, even love, for the oddly-shaped suitor she has spurned.

Part of Edward Lear's genius is the mingling of Victorian romantic dreams of exploration and exotica – the Coast of Coromandel, the silent-roaring ocean – with the bourgeois preoccupations equally typical of the age – the price of prawns, the correct title of Mr. Jones' business, the preoccupation with "worldly goods" as a prerequisite for marriage. He puts it all into resounding language that is both a tribute to, and an affectionate mockery of, his friend Tennyson.

Lear was epileptic, and, in his own opinion, too ugly to attract a mate. He poured out affection on his friends and on Old Foss, his cat, but remained single and melancholy all his life. It is hard not to see a self-portrait in the poor dear Yonghy-Bonghy-Bo.

When as the Rie

BY GEORGE PEELE 1556–1596
Song from THE OLD WIVES' TALE 1595

When as the Rie reach to the chin,
And chopcherrie chopcherrie ripe within,
Strawberries swimming in the creame,
And schoole boyes playing in the streame:
Then O, then O, then O my true love said
Till that time come againe,
Shee could not live a maid.

Who could fail to smile at this unabashed response to the most sensual time of year? The rye crop is tall enough to conceal tumbling lovers, the strawberries and the schoolboys are interchangeably energetic, and the ratio of strawberries to cream sounds good to me.

"Chop-cherry" is a flirtatious game in which you take it in turns to bite dangling cherries with your hands behind your back, and "ripe within" – well, that's what this little ditty is all about. The "true love" is certainly ripe within; she is not going to put up with her virgin state any longer. Cresta liked the fact it was she who was making the running. Reading aloud, I wasn't quite brave enough to give the "O"s the full Meg Ryan treatment, but I'm sure that's what's meant.

George Peele was Shakespeare's contemporary, and may have collaborated with him on *Titus Andronicus*, which features chopping of a rather different kind. This song comes from Peele's play *The Old Wives' Tale*, a satire of romantic drama containing a fairy-tale play-within-a-play. The *Tale* has the first-ever use of "duck" (as a term of endearment, not a waterfowl), and "booby". It also contains the line "Fee fa fum, here comes an Englishman", forerunner of the Ogre's chant in Jack and the Beanstalk. But I digress.

Bryd one Brere

ANON., c.1300

Bryd one brere, brid, brid one brere,
Kynd is come of love, love to crave
Blythful biryd, on me thu rewe
Or greyth, lef, greith thu me my grave.

Hic am so blithe, so bryhit, brid on brere,
Quan I se that hende in halle:
Yhe is whit of lime, loveli, trewe
Yhe is fayr and flur of alle.

Mikte ic hire at wille haven,
Stedefast of love, loveli, trewe,
Of mi sorwe yhe may me saven
Ioye and blisse were were me newe.

Possibly the oldest love-lyric in English. Here is my unscholarly version:

> Bird on a briar, bright bird on a briar,
> Love made us, so love we crave.
> Bird full of bliss, have mercy on me
> Or dig, gladly dig for me my grave.
>
> I am as blithe, as bright as a bird on a briar
> When I see that handmaiden in the hall:
> She is white of limb, lovely, true
> She is the fairest and the flower of all.
>
> If I might have her at my will,
> Steadfast in love, lovely, true,
> She could save me from my sorrow
> Joy and bliss would me renew.

The words were written on the back of a papal bull issued by Pope Innocent III in 1199, probably about a hundred years later. I don't think there's any connection between the contents of the bull and "Bryd one Brere"; it's the medieval equivalent of George Harrison scribbling "Here Comes the Sun" on the back of an envelope.

This is clearly meant to be sung. We couldn't quite rise to that, but Sue read it aloud in her resonant Middle English voice, and we were all touched by its fresh and delicate poignancy. "This calls to us down the ages," said Sue; "I particularly love the early poets – even though they're anonymous, their thoughts and feelings, sorrows, anxieties and joys make them so instantly recognisable, so like ourselves."

Magnificat

BY MICHÈLE ROBERTS 1949–

(*For Sian, after thirteen years*)

oh this man
what a meal he made of me
how he chewed and gobbled and sucked

in the end he spat me all out

you arrived on the dot, in the nick
of time, with your red curls flying
I was about to slip down the sink like grease
I nearly collapsed, I almost
wiped myself out like a stain
I called for you, and you came, you voyaged
fierce as a small archangel with swords and breasts
you declared the birth of a new life
in my kitchen there was an annunciation
and I was still, awed by your hair's glory

you commanded me to sing of my redemption

oh my friend, how
you were mother for me, and how
I could let myself lean on you

comfortable as an old cloth, familiar as enamel
   saucepans
I was a child again, pyjamaed
in winceyette, my hair plaited, and you
listened, you soothed me like cakes and milk
you listened to me for three days, and I poured
it out, I flowed all over you like wine, like oil, you
   touched the place where it hurt
at night we slept together in my big bed
your shoulder eased me towards dreams

when we met, I tell you
it was a birthday party, a funeral
it was a holy communion
between women, a Visitation

it was two old she-goats butting
and nuzzling each other in the smelly fold

Michèle Roberts had a Roman Catholic mother, attended
a convent school, and even at one point expected to
become a nun, before losing her faith as an undergraduate; her use of religious imagery to express intense experience is hardly surprising. She has spoken of "the nun

in my head, that monstrous Mother Superior", but in "Magnificat" the arrival of her friend, the "small arch-angel", is entirely a blessing. Roberts draws on St Luke's account of two visits; the Angel Gabriel telling the Virgin Mary that she will give birth to Jesus, and Mary's subsequent visit to her elderly cousin Elizabeth, already miraculously pregnant with John the Baptist. She treats her source material with creative flexibility; she empha-sises the domestic snugness of the two women closeted together at a crucial time in their lives, preparing for "the birth of a new life", and exploits the richness of bibli-cal and liturgical language and imagery – annunciation, redemption, holy communion, glory, song, flying, swords, wine, oil, even goats. But both Roberts and the reader are free to take the bits they want and reject the rest. The two women in the poem brush against Mary, Elizabeth and Gabriel, but no laborious parallel is drawn.

We agreed that the poem fuses many aspects of female experience – motherhood, daughterhood, friend-ship, erotic connection. "Slipping down the sink like grease is a brilliant way of describing complete loss of self-esteem," said Sarah N. We relished the familiarity of winceyette pyjamas and enamel saucepans, and the way this ordinary domestic environment is blessed and elevated by the arrival of love.

Sonnet Written in the Churchyard at Middleton in Sussex

BY CHARLOTTE SMITH 1749–1806

Pressed by the Moon, mute arbitress of tides,
While the loud equinox its power combines,
The sea no more its swelling surge confines,
But o'er the shrinking land sublimely rides.
The wild blast, rising from the western cave,
Drives the huge billows from their heaving bed;
Tears from their grassy tombs the village dead,
And breaks the silent sabbath of the grave!
With shells and sea-weed mingled, on the shore,
Lo! their bones whiten in the frequent wave;
But vain to them the winds and waters rave;
They hear the warring elements no more:
While I am doomed, by life's long storm oppressed,
To gaze with envy on their gloomy rest.

Charlotte Smith's costume-drama of a life story proves that truth is stranger than fiction. Married off at 14 so that she would be out of the way of her new step-mother – a manoeuvre that Charlotte later described as "legal prostitution" – she soon discovered that her husband Benjamin was extravagant, profligate, violent and faithless. His father had been a rich West India merchant, but litigation over the disposal of his fortune was so complicated that Charlotte was plagued by it for the rest of her life; it's thought to be the model for the interminable lawsuit "Jarndyce v. Jarndyce" in Dickens' *Bleak House*. Benjamin's misuse of his trust fund led to his imprisonment; Charlotte, by now the mother of several children, joined him in jail. On his release they decamped to Dieppe to avoid his creditors, and Charlotte turned to writing and translating to earn money. Eventually she achieved a separation from the unreformable Benjamin; this sonnet was written at about this time. "I wrote mournfully because I was unhappy," she said.

She had literary friends, and they helped her, but she depended on writing to support herself and her nine children. The poet William Cowper (see page 286) described her as "Chain'd to her desk like a slave to his oar". Some of her many novels dealt with radical politics, which led to a suspicion that she was a spy. Wordsworth, at first a keen supporter of the French Revolution, called on Charlotte on his way to France in 1791 and found her a fellow enthusiast, though in later years both poets changed their views. Wordsworth thought highly of the mixture of close natural observation and self-scrutiny in her poetry, but his good opinion could not save her from near destitution at the end of her life, when she was too ill to hold a pen. Her estranged husband died in prison.

Charlotte Smith is credited with reviving the sonnet form, which had fallen out of fashion, but was eagerly taken up by the Romantic poets including Wordsworth himself. In the Middleton Churchyard sonnet, she describes a graveyard on the sea's edge near Midhurst in Sussex where she was then living; storms had torn the graves open and human remains lay scattered on the shore.

A Birthday

BY CHRISTINA ROSSETTI 1830–1894

My heart is like a singing bird
 Whose nest is in a water'd shoot;
My heart is like an apple-tree
 Whose boughs are bent with thickset fruit;
My heart is like a rainbow shell
 That paddles in a halcyon sea;
My heart is gladder than all these
 Because my love is come to me.

Raise me a dais of silk and down;
 Hang it with vair and purple dyes;
Carve it in doves and pomegranates,
 And peacocks with a hundred eyes;
Work it in gold and silver grapes,
 In leaves and silver fleurs-de-lys;
Because the birthday of my life
 Is come, my love is come to me.

One of the pleasures of poetry is that it makes you presents of new words. "Vair" is red squirrel fur, used for trimming gorgeous medieval robes. Much of Christina Rossetti's verse is sombre and melancholy, but this one is a blaze of triumph. "It's like a word version of one of her brother's [Dante Gabriel Rossetti's] paintings," said Kirsty.

Sarah F, recalling Rossetti's much-anthologised sonnet "Remember", said that when she was a teenager her mother gave her a collection of Rossetti's poems. "'Remember' feels like the threads of a spider's web that link me to the past. The repetition of 'Remember me' is hypnotic and round like the outer traces of the web; and the sounds of the 't' and the 'f' in the line, 'Better by far you should forget and smile' and the long 'i' in 'smile' carry me into the distance." "A Birthday" also achieves a hypnotic effect, through the regular repetition of "My heart" in the first stanza and the queenly, single-syllable commands of the second: "raise", "hang", "work". And the large, open vowel sounds are as magnificent as the throne they describe.

I Had a Little Nut Tree

ANON., c.1506

I had a little nut tree
Nothing would it bear
But a silver nutmeg
And a golden pear.
The King of Spain's daughter
Came to visit me
And all for the sake of
My little nut tree.
I skipped over water
I danced over sea
And all the birds in the air
Couldn't catch me.

Nursery rhymes furnish our infant selves with the rhythms, the rhymes, the characters, the roomscapes and the landscapes which are the basis of so much of our creativity and psychological security. To deny nursery rhymes to a child is a form of sensory deprivation. The best nursery rhymes are poetry in its purest form, where the sound of the words is its own meaning, and where nothing has to be explained.

Dating nursery rhymes is interesting but difficult. "I Had a Little Nut Tree'" may date to 1506, when Mad Joanna of Castile, daughter of Ferdinand and Isabella, was sent to the court of Henry VII of England as a potential bride for one of his sons; indeed, Cresta grew up with "came to marry me", not "visit me". Then again, it may not. In any event, the silver nutmeg and the golden pear hang shining with entrancing beauty, and skipping over water and dancing over sea is a supremely desirable activity, the ultimate liberation.

9

WAR

"Arma virumque cano" – "Of arms and the man I sing." That is how Virgil opened his *Aeneid* in about 30 BC. War has always been a dominant subject for poets, but the nature of "war poetry" was changed radically, and probably for ever, by the colossal and universal suffering of the First World War.

The Day Is A Poem – September 19, 1939

BY ROBINSON JEFFERS 1887–1962

This morning Hitler spoke in Danzig, we hear his voice.
A man of genius: that is, of amazing
Ability, courage, devotion, cored on a sick child's soul,
Heard clearly through the dog wrath, a sick child
Wailing in Danzig; invoking destruction and wailing at it.
Here, the day was extremely hot; about noon
A south wind like a blast from hell's mouth spilled a slight
    rain
On the parched land, and at five a light earthquake
Danced the house, no harm done. Tonight I have been
    amusing myself
Watching the blood-red moon droop slowly
Into the black sea through bursts of dry lightning and
    distant thunder.
Well: the day is a poem: but too much
Like one of Jeffers's, crusted with blood and barbaric
    omens,
Painful to excess, inhuman as a hawk's cry.

Robinson Jeffers awaits the end of the world in the granite house he built near Carmel, California, with its secret staircase and "hawk tower". Hitler is as yet only a partly known quantity, but Jeffers' assessment of him is prescient. "A sick child wailing," said Judith, "that's exactly right." Jeffers can hear Hitler, not see him; the voice, the "dog wrath", which links to the "blast from hell's mouth" and the hawk's cry, sends shock waves through the listener and through the world. The heat, the earthquake, the blood-red moon, the black sea... nature seems infected by the same sickness. You can watch a YouTube recording of this very speech.

Jeffers opposed American involvement in the war on environmentalist grounds. As a result, his poetry fell from favour. He wrote of "inhumanism", believing that our obsession with the works of Man and materialism prevented us from seeing the wholeness of the world, "the astonishing beauty of things". Through the twenties and thirties he wrote brutal, apocalyptic poetry, full of foreboding. Now, on this September day when the elements of human and natural destructiveness come together in a dance of death, it seems that his poetic prophecies are coming true.

Roman Wall Blues

BY W.H. AUDEN 1907–1973

Over the heather the wet wind blows,
I've lice in my tunic and a cold in my nose.

The rain comes pattering out of the sky,
I'm a Wall soldier, I don't know why.

The mist creeps over the hard grey stone,
My girl's in Tungria; I sleep alone.

Aulus goes hanging around her place,
I don't like his manners, I don't like his face.

Piso's a Christian, he worships a fish;
There'd be no kissing if he had his wish.

She gave me a ring but I diced it away;
I want my girl and I want my pay.

When I'm a veteran with only one eye
I shall do nothing but look at the sky.

The complaint of the rank and file soldier, unchanged in two thousand years: homesick, sex-starved, a cog in an incomprehensible machine. Auden probably had the Hadrian's Wall fort Housesteads in mind; it was garrisoned by Tungrians, tribesmen from the Belgic part of Gaul. Our soldier has been pressed into service. He has no special interest in, or loyalty to, Rome. "We're here because we're here because we're here."

He's neither hero nor villain; an ordinary man with ordinary concerns, ordinary failings. He loves his girl but he lets her down. He wants his pay, but there's a strong chance he'll waste it. He grumbles about discomfort, but he's not going to run away; he'll end his service with "only one eye", having put up with whatever happens to you when you're a soldier. The eternal irony is that the fighting man is, essentially, powerless.

Sue said she wouldn't blame the girl for thinking Aulus was a better bet. Sarah N, about to go on a walking holiday along Hadrian's Wall, said she would now see it as populated by spirits from the past. Auden's most obvious success is to have made history come to life in the form of this very believable soldier. But he is also writing about man's need for belief, the urge to find a meaning for existence. The soldier sounds scornful of Piso the Christian, but he's noticed him; there's a grudging curiosity, a latent desire to make sense of things. In old age he'll keep his one remaining eye not on the ground, but on the sky.

There's a bleak beauty in the wind, the mist, the hard grey stone, a sombre permanence as a backdrop to human life.

Parting in Wartime
BY FRANCES CORNFORD 1886–1960

How long ago Hector took off his plume,
Not wanting that his little son should cry,
Then kissed his sad Andromache goodbye –
And now we three in Euston waiting-room.

In one of the most touchingly human moments of the
Iliad, the great Trojan warrior Hector bids farewell to
his loving and loyal wife Andromache and baby son
Astyanax before going off to fight. Astyanax is frightened
by his father's plumed helmet, so Hector takes it off, and
places the little boy in the comfort of Andromache's
arms. Twenty-six centuries later, Frances Cornford's
husband says goodbye to her and their small son John as
he sets off to fight in the First World War. Her husband
(Francis with an i) was a classical scholar, which is an
additional reason for drawing the Homeric parallel, but
the poem's simple message is legible without any background information. "You're there in the waiting-room
with them," said Polly.

John grew up to be a poet himself. He was killed in the
Spanish Civil War, fighting against the Fascists.

From a Full Heart

BY A.A. MILNE 1882–1956

In days of peace my fellow-men
Rightly regarded me as more like
A Bishop than a Major-Gen.,
And nothing since has made me warlike;
But when this agelong struggle ends
And I have seen the Allies dish up
The goose of Hindenburg – oh, friends!
I shall out-bish the mildest Bishop.

When the War is over and the Kaiser's out of print,
I'm going to buy some tortoises and watch the
    beggars sprint;
When the War is over and the sword at last we
    sheathe,
I'm going to keep a jelly-fish and listen to it breathe.

I never really longed for gore,
And any taste for red corpuscles
That lingered with me left before
The German troops had entered Brussels.
In early days the Colonel's "Shun!"
Froze me; and, as the War grew older,
The noise of someone else's gun
Left me considerably colder.

When the War is over and the battle has been won,
I'm going to buy a barnacle and take it for a run;
When the War is over and the German Fleet we
    sink,
I'm going to keep a silk-worm's egg and listen to it
    think.

The Captains and the Kings depart –
It may be so, but not lieutenants;
Dawn after weary dawn I start
The never-ending round of penance;
One rock amid the welter stands
On which my gazed is fixed intently –
An after-life in quiet hands
Lived very lazily and gently.

When the war is over and we've done the Belgians
    proud,
I'm going to keep a chrysalis and read to it aloud;
When the War is over and we've finished up the
    show,
I'm going to plant a lemon-pip and listen to it grow.

Oh, I'm tired of the noise and the turmoil of battle,
And I'm even upset by the lowing of cattle,
And the clang of the bluebells is death to my liver,
And the roar of the dandelion gives me a shiver,
And a glacier, in movement, is much too exciting,

And I'm nervous, when standing on one, of alighting —
Give me Peace; that is all, that is all that I seek...
Say, starting on Saturday week.

Yes, a war poem of a kind from the creator of Winnie the Pooh. A.A. Milne was a 2nd Lieutenant with the Royal Warwickshire Regiment and was wounded on the seventh day of the Battle of the Somme. Everyone warmed to this one. I defy you not to.

Pillbox

BY EDMUND BLUNDEN 1896–1974

Just see what's happening, Worley – Worley rose
And round the angled doorway thrust his nose
And Sergeant Hoad went, too, to snuff the air.
Then war brought down his fist, and missed the pair!
Yet Hoad was scratched by a splinter, the blood came,
And out burst terrors that he'd striven to tame,
A good man, Hoad, for weeks. *I'm blown to bits*,
He groans, he screams. *Come Bluffer, where's your wits?*
Says Worley. *Bluffer, you've a blighty, man!*
All in the pillbox urged him, here began
His freedom: *Think of Eastbourne and your dad.*
The poor man lay at length and brief and mad
Flung out his cry of doom; soon ebbed and dumb
He yielded. Worley with a tot of rum
And shouting in his face could not restore him.
The ship of Charon over channel bore him.
All marvelled even on that most deadly day
To see this life so spirited away.

"Pillbox" is one of the very few poems of the First World
War that names individual soldiers. I was particularly

interested in it because Sergeant Hoad came from the Battle area, where I live, and it's a distinctive local surname. "I nearly fell off my chair when you gave us this," said Polly. "I had never seen it before and the mention of Sergeant Hoad was amazing as my maiden name was Hoad. I went home, and found out that Blunden's Sergeant Hoad was my grandfather's cousin. Thank you for discovering a poetic link in my family!"

Frank Worley, the other named soldier, was also real. He was a young butcher from Worthing. Edmund Blunden fought alongside both men in the 11th Battalion of the Royal Sussex Regiment. In his memoir *Undertones of War*, Blunden praises Worley's "calmness and kindness". One evening, Worley brewed cocoa for Blunden over a fire made from shreds of sandbags and ends of tallow candle. As Blunden took the mug, two hand grenades burst on the parapet behind them. Worley was as "undiverted as though a butterfly or two had settled on a flower".

The incident described in "Pillbox" is also recounted in *Undertones of War*. Poor Sergeant Hoad, venturing outside the pillbox, is only slightly wounded, but he dies because he believes he's going to die, and all Worley's humanity cannot restore him.

After the war, Blunden and Worley lost touch, until Worley heard about Blunden's book in 1929 and made contact. They remained friends until Worley's death in 1954. Blunden inscribed a copy of the book for Worley's daughter Margaret: "Through this book, something of his personality has been understood by many who have never met him."

Tim Worley, his great-nephew, has his medal and citation "for most conspicuous gallantry and devotion to duty". I am grateful to Tim for additional information about his great-uncle's life.

Easter Monday

BY ELEANOR FARJEON 1881–1965

In the last letter that I had from France
You thanked me for the silver Easter egg
Which I had hidden in the box of apples
You liked to munch beyond all other fruit.
You found the egg the Monday before Easter,
And said "I will praise Easter Monday now –
It was such a lovely morning." Then you spoke
Of the coming battle and said, "This is the eve.
Goodbye. And may I have a letter soon."

That Easter Monday was a day for praise,
It was such a lovely morning. In our garden
We sowed our earliest seeds, and in the orchard
The apple-bud was ripe. It was the eve.
There are three letters that you will not get.

In the autumn of 1912, shy, bespectacled Eleanor Farjeon met the writer Edward Thomas. They became close
friends; Farjeon was probably in love with the very handsome Thomas, but would have regarded him as out of

her league, and in any case he was married, albeit not happily. They met for long walks, and exchanged frequent letters. When the Great War broke out, Thomas did not immediately enlist – he was already in his late thirties, above recruitment age, and married with young children – but in 1915 he changed his mind. As they walked together on the Sussex Downs, Farjeon asked him why he'd joined up. Thomas picked up a handful of earth, crumbled it, and replied, "Literally, for this."

He was killed by a shell blast at Arras on Easter Monday 1917. When she heard the news, Eleanor Farjeon wrote this poem. His letters to her survive, hers to him do not, though I suppose "Easter Monday" is a letter to his memory.

Breakfast

BY WILFRID WILSON GIBSON, OCTOBER 1914

We ate our breakfast lying on our backs,
Because the shells were screeching overhead.
I bet a rasher to a loaf of bread
That Hull United would beat Halifax
When Jimmy Stainthorpe played full-back instead
Of Billy Bradford. Ginger raised his head
And cursed, and took the bet; and dropt back dead.
We ate our breakfast lying on our backs,
Because the shells were screeching overhead.

Wilfrid Gibson volunteered for the Army but was rejected four times on health grounds. Eventually he joined the Army Service Corps Motor Transport. "Breakfast" was based on a soldier's anecdote. "It's so simple, and so shocking," said Pepe, "it's like a body blow."

"Breakfast" is an admirable exercise in compression, but Wilson could also sustain feeling throughout a long poem, as in his creepy "Flannan Isle", which tells the story of a haunted lighthouse, and is the one poem that Mike F remembered with pleasure from his schooldays.

my sweet old etcetera

BY E E CUMMINGS 1894–1962

my sweet old etcetera
aunt lucy during the recent

war could and what
is more did tell you just
what everybody was fighting

for,
my sister

isabel created hundreds
(and
hundreds) of socks not to
mention shirts fleaproof earwarmers

etcetera wristers etcetera, my
mother hoped that

i would die etcetera
bravely of course my father used
to become hoarse talking about how it was
a privilege and if only he
could meanwhile my

self etcetera lay quietly
in the deep mud et

cetera
(dreaming,
et
cetera, of
Your smile
eyes knees and of your Etcetera)

Despite his anti-war views, cummings joined the Ambu-
lance Corps in 1917 and served in France. He was
arrested on suspicion of espionage and held in a military
detention camp.

Expanding on the etceteras proved entertaining and
instructive. "It's not so much reading between the lines,
as reading around the words," said David.

Falling Asleep

BY SIEGFRIED SASSOON 1886–1967

Voices moving about in the quiet house:
Thud of feet and a muffled shutting of doors;
Everyone yawning. Only the clocks are alert.

Out in the night there's autumn-smelling gloom
Crowded with whispering trees; across the park
A hollow cry of hounds like lonely bells:
And I know that the clouds are moving across the moon;
The low, red, rising moon. Now herons call
And wrangle by their pool; and hooting owls
Sail from the wood above pale stooks of oats.

Waiting for sleep, I drift from thoughts like these;
And where to-day was dream-like, build my dreams.
Music... there was a bright white room below,
And someone singing a song about a soldier,
One hour, two hours ago: and soon the song
Will be "last night": but now the beauty swings
Across my brain, ghost of remembered chords
Which still can make such radiance in my dream
That I can watch the marching of my soldiers,
And count their faces; faces; sunlit faces.

Falling asleep... the herons, and the hounds...

September in the darkness; and the world
I've known; all fading past me into peace.

Sassoon's heroism both as a soldier and as an oppo-
nent of the way the First World War was conducted are
extremely well known, as is his bitter, uncompromising
war poetry. This poem, written ten months after the
Armistice, shows him processing the knowledge that
the fighting is over, and that he can return to something
resembling a peaceful life. The beloved Kentish landscape of his youth is still there. Time passes, and makes
repairs. He can dare to think of the men he commanded
not as corpses in waiting, but as men with sunlit faces,
men who can be transformed and immortalised in a
beautiful song.

"I'm glad he wrote this," said Polly. "He deserved it."

10

LANDSCAPES & CITYSCAPES

The poems in this section show the poet as a painter in words, selecting and highlighting certain details to bring out mood and meaning.

A September Night

BY GEORGE MARION MCCLELLAN 1860–1934

The full September moon sheds floods of light,
And all the bayou's face is gemmed with stars,
Save where are dropped fantastic shadows down
From sycamores and moss-hung cypress trees.
With slumberous sound the waters half asleep
Creep on and on their way, 'twixt rankish reeds,
Through marsh and lowlands stretching to the Gulf.
Begirt with cotton fields, Anguilla sits
Half bird-like, dreaming on her Summer nest.
Amid her spreading figs and roses, still
In bloom with all their Spring and Summer hues,
Pomegranates hang with dapple cheeks full ripe,
And over all the town a dreamy haze
Drops down. The great plantations, stretching far
Away, are plains of cotton, downy white.
O, glorious is this night of joyous sounds;
Too full for sleep. Aromas wild and sweet,
From muscadine, late blooming jessamine,
And roses, all the heavy air suffuse.
Faint bellows from the alligators come
From swamps afar, where sluggish lagoons give
To them a peaceful home. The katydids
Make ceaseless cries. Ten thousand insects' wings
Stir in the moonlight haze and joyous shouts

Of Negro song and mirth awake hard by
The cabin dance. O, glorious is this night!
The Summer sweetness fills my heart with songs
I can not sing, with loves I can not speak.

This slow, careful, sumptuous word picture was written by a black teacher and Congregational minister and published in his collection *A Path of Dreams*. It's fascinating to find a Mississippi landscape described in a style that owes much to the English Romantics. But it's no mere pastiche; with the "fantastic" shadows of the Spanish moss, the bellowing alligators and the muscadine, McClellan makes the subject his own. "It's got a lovely mellow shadowy quality," said Pam, seeing it in her mind's eye.

The plains of cotton and the "Negro" cabin are presented without overt political comment. It feels as if McClellan's intention is to celebrate and dignify the workers by showing the intensity of their response to the glorious September night; choosing to write in blank verse using elevated poetic diction adds to that dignity. "It's interesting that he wants us to see the cotton fields as beautiful," said Veronica. "He particularly wants us to notice them because he mentions them twice." Sarah N thought that we might interpret the last two lines very differently if the poet was white: "Knowing he's black means we inevitably see a kind of double meaning in them."

Anguilla is a small town in Sharkey County, Mississippi. A century after the publication of this poem, Paul Theroux described it in very different terms in his travelogue *Deep South*: "...desolate, a scattering of mobile homes on the edge of the road and bordering the ploughed fields – decayed, rusted boxes, lying higgledy-piggledy with an air of disorder and desperation, like a refugee camp."

Hurrahing in Harvest

BY GERARD MANLEY HOPKINS 1844–1889

Summer ends now; now, barbarous in beauty, the stooks
   arise
Around; up above, what wind-walks! what lovely
   behaviour
Of silk-sack clouds! has wilder, wilful-wavier
Meal-drift moulded ever and melted across skies?

I walk, I lift up, I lift up heart, eyes,
Down all that glory in the heavens to glean our Saviour;
And, eyes, heart, what looks, what lips yet gave you a
Rapturous love's greeting of realer, of rounder replies?

And the azurous hung hills are his world-wielding
   shoulder
Majestic – as a stallion stalwart, very-violet-sweet! –
These things, these things were here and but the beholder
Wanting; which two when they once meet,
The heart rears wings bold and bolder
And hurls for him, O half hurls earth for him off under
   his feet.

This glad shout of praise was written not long after Hopkins broke his seven years' self-imposed poetic silence. On becoming a Jesuit he burnt all his verses (or thought he did – a few survived) in an attempt at ascetic self-discipline. Seven years later, thankfully for posterity, the head of the theological college where Hopkins was studying wisely asked him to write a poem commemorating the death of five Franciscan nuns in a shipwreck. The result was the remarkable "The Wreck of the Deutschland", far too long to be included here.

Liberated by this priestly permission, Hopkins then poured out a series of ecstatic sonnets which explore his belief that the natural world was "word, expression, news of God". Sue, who is a Roman Catholic, truly understood what Hopkins meant about "gleaning our Saviour"; "this poem gloriously confirms and celebrates the sublime, mutual love of almighty God and his rapturous beholder. I absolutely love it." But even the most hardened atheist can warm to the exuberant originality of Hopkins' response.

The Soote Season

BY HENRY HOWARD, EARL OF SURREY 1516/17–1547

The soote season, that bud and blome furth bringes,
With grene hath clad the hill and eke the vale;
The nightingale with fethers new she singes;
The turtle to her make hath told her tale:
Somer is come, for every spray nowe springes,
The hart hath hong his olde hed on the pale:
The buck in brake his winter cote he flinges:
The fishes flote with newe repaired scale:
The adder all her sloughe away she slinges:
The swift swalow pursueth the flyes smale:
The busy bee her honye now she minges:
Winter is worne that was the flowers bale:
And thus I see among these pleasant thinges
Eche care decayes, and yet my sorow springes.

The premise here is simple, and conventional. In the
sweet ("soote") spring season, everything bursts into
bloom, birds sing, beasts cast off their winter lethargy, the
earth rejoices – all except the unhappy speaker, whose
"sorow" grows in vigorous proportion. We are not told

the cause of the sorrow, but we assume that it's unfulfilled desire, because this poem belongs so clearly to the lyric tradition of unhappy lovers. Surrey uses the new-fangled, Italianate sonnet form, but the mood, the use of alliteration and the simple vocabulary belong to Middle English – see "Bryd one Brere" on page 202. A line like "The hart hath hong his olde hed on the pale" could have come straight out of the 14th century. There's no argument here, no intellectual challenge, just a dense evocation of teeming, buzzing fertility.

Judith loved the rich biodiversity, the way Surrey includes adders, flies and fish as well as the more expected deer and nightingales. By calling attention to skin and scales he makes us feel the physicality of the process of renewal. We talked wistfully about turtle doves telling their tales of love to their "makes" [mates, pairs], their churring noise once the essence of early summer but now almost vanished, and the nightingale not far behind.

Surrey was "the most foolish proud boy that is in England", according to one of the King's clerics, and his pride was his undoing. Like his friend and fellow poet Sir Thomas Wyatt (see page 105), he was cast into the Tower – not, like Wyatt, for pursuing Anne Boleyn (who was his first cousin) but for "treasonably" quartering his coat-of-arms with those of Edward the Confessor. He was executed on 19 January 1547, aged about 30, only a few days before the death of Henry VIII himself.

Last Snow

BY ANDREW YOUNG 1885–1971

Although the snow still lingers
Heaped on the ivy's blunt webbed fingers
And painting tree-trunks on one side,
Here in this sunlit ride
The fresh unchristened things appear,
Leaf, spathe and stem,
With crumbs of earth clinging to them
To show the way they came
But no flower yet to tell their name,
And one green spear
Stabbing a dead leaf from below
Kills winter at a blow.

Andrew Young was rector of Stonegate in East Sussex, where we live, which gave us a friendly feeling about him. He observed nature closely, as is the wont of the Anglican clergy, and turned his observations into unobtrusive but emphatic poems. Here he records that exact moment when winter turns to spring, when you suddenly notice last year's thin brown leaf impaled on a new green spike. "The arrivals are 'unchristened' because he can't yet name them," said Michael W. The distinctive appearance of each plant hasn't yet unfurled, but what Young does understand is "the way they came". This is a poem about Christian faith, in the lowest possible key.

A Nocturnal Reverie

BY ANNE FINCH, COUNTESS OF WINCHELSEA 1661–1720

In such a night, when every louder wind
Is to its distant cavern safe confined;
And only gentle Zephyr fans his wings,
And lonely Philomel, still waking, sings;
Or from some tree, famed for the owl's delight,
She, hollowing clear, directs the wanderer right;
In such a night, when passing clouds give place,
Or thinly veil the heaven's mysterious face;
When in some river overhung with green,
The waving moon and trembling leaves are seen;
When freshened grass now bears itself upright,
And makes cool banks to pleasing rest invite,
Whence springs the woodbind and the bramble-rose,
And where the sleepy cowslip sheltered grows;
Whilst now a paler hue the foxglove takes,
Yet chequers still with red the dusky brakes;
When scattered glow-worms, but in twilight fine,
Show trivial beauties, watch their hour to shine;
Whilst Salisb'ry stands the test of every light,
In perfect charms and perfect virtue bright;
When odours, which declined repelling day,
Through temperate air uninterrupted stray;
When darkened groves their softest shadows wear,

And falling waters we distinctly hear;
When through the gloom more venerable shows
Some ancient fabric, awful in repose,
While sunburnt hills their swarthy looks conceal,
And swelling haycocks thicken up the vale;
When the loosed horse now, as his pasture leads,
Comes slowly grazing through th'adjoining meads,
Whose stealing pace and lengthened shade we fear,
Till torn-up forage in his teeth we hear;
When nibbling sheep at large pursue their food,
And unmolested kine rechew the cud;
When curlews cry beneath the village walls,
And to her straggling brood the partridge calls;
Their short-lived jubilee the creatures keep,
Which but endures whilst tyrant man does sleep;
When a sedate content the spirit feels,
And no fierce light disturbs, whilst it reveals,
But silent musings urge the mind to seek
Something too high for syllables to speak;
Till the free soul to a compos'dness charmed,
Finding the elements of rage disarmed,
O'er all below a solemn quiet grown,
Joys in th'inferior world and thinks it like her own:
In such a night let me abroad remain,
Till morning breaks, and all's confused again:
Our cares, our toils, our clamours are renewed,
Or pleasures, seldom reached, again pursued.

When I read this aloud, stumbling somewhat, Amanda exclaimed sympathetically, "It's all one long sentence!" Indeed, there are no full stops. Anne Finch guides us gently through the darkling landscape; her semi-colons (my own favourite punctuation mark), like stiles, allow us pauses for breath. It is not a poem made to be declaimed, but rather, as its title suggests, one to be quietly internalised.

Everyone took an instant liking to Anne Finch, partly because a female voice from the age of Pope and Swift is refreshing, partly because her details are so easy to see, hear and feel. Darkness enhances the senses.

We read it in mid-June, the day after a full moon. "It's now!" said Sarah N. "Or perhaps a couple of weeks ago... there are still some cowslips, but the foxgloves are out, and the partridges have chicks." Shelagh loved the "waving" moon reflected in the river, Veronica the "freshened" grass, sorting itself out after a drooping day of heat. Polly was charmed by the horse, who changes from a long-shadowed monster creeping up behind us into a friendly old dobbin once we can hear him munching the "torn-up forage".

"Jubilee" is an interesting word. According to Leviticus, it's the time when, every seven years, farmers in Israel must let their land lie fallow, when slaves and prisoners are freed, debts are forgiven, and God's mercies are made particularly manifest. Anne Finch watches the creatures enjoy a few hours of freedom – their "short-lived jubilee" – from the demands of "tyrant man". She makes no direct mention of God, but describes her nocturnal communion with the natural world as a transcendent, spiritual experience, "something too high for syllables to speak". It comes as no surprise that Wordsworth rated her poetry very highly.

London's Summer Morning

BY MARY "PERDITA" ROBINSON 1757–1800

Who hast not waked to list the busy sounds
Of summer's morning, in the sultry smoke
Of noisy London? On the pavement hot
The sooty chimney-boy, with dingy face
And tatter'd covering, shrilly bawls his trade,
Rousing the sleepy housemaid. At the door
The milk-pail rattles, and the tinkling bell
Proclaims the dustman's office; while the street
Is lost in clouds impervious. Now begins
The din of hackney-coaches, waggons, carts;
While tinmen's shops, and noisy trunk-makers,
Knife-grinders, coopers, squeaking cork-cutters,
Fruit barrows, and the hunger-giving cries
Of vegetable vendors, fill the air.
Now every shop displays its varied trade,
And the fresh-sprinkled pavement cools the feet
Of early walkers. At the private door
The ruddy housemaid twirls the busy mop,
Annoying the smart 'prentice, or neat girl,
Tripping with band-box lightly. Now the sun
Darts burning splendour on the glittering pane,
Save where the canvas awning throws a shade
On the gay merchandise. Now, spruce and trim,
In shops (where beauty smiles with industry),

Sits the smart damsel; while the passenger
Peeps through the window, watching every charm.
Now pastry dainties catch the eye minute
Of humming insects, while the limy snare
Waits to entral them. Now the lamplighter
Mounts the tall ladder, nimbly venturous,
To trim the half-fill'd lamp; while at his feet
The pot-boy yells discordant! All along
The sultry pavement, the old-clothes man cries
In tone monotonous, then side-long views
The area for his traffic: now the bag
Is slily open'd, and the half-worn suit
(Sometimes the pilfer'd treasure of the base
Domestic spoiler), for one half its worth,
Sinks in the green abyss. The porter now
Bears his huge load along the burning way;
And the poor poet wakes from busy dreams,
To paint the summer morning.

The beautiful Mary Robinson was generally known as "Perdita" after she played that role to great acclaim in *The Winter's Tale*. In the audience was the Prince of Wales, future Prince Regent and King George IV, who offered her £20,000 to become his mistress. Perdita had endured years of financial difficulty with her feckless, useless husband; she first started writing poetry when in debtor's jail with him and her beloved six-month-old daughter. She succumbed to "Prinny". Alas, the cash never materialised. When, in the spirited "London's Summer Morning", she writes of "the poor poet", she speaks from experience.

Perdita was memorably painted by the greatest portrait artists of her day – Gainsborough, Romney, Reynolds. Her own pen portrait of a London street scene is no mean feat.

Nightfall in the City of Hyderabad
BY SAROJINI NAIDU 1879–1949

See how the speckled sky burns like a pigeon's throat,
Jewelled with embers of opal and peridote.

See the white river that flashes and scintillates,
Curved like a tusk from the mouth of the city-gates.

Hark, from the minaret, how the muezzin's call
Floats like a battle-flag over the city wall.

From trellised balconies, languid and luminous
Faces gleam, veiled in a splendour voluminous.

Leisurely elephants wind through the winding lanes,
Swinging their silver bells hung from their silver chains.

Round the high Char Minar sounds of gay cavalcades
Blend with the music of cymbals and serenades.

Over the city bridge Night comes majestical,
Borne like a queen to a sumptuous festival.

Sarojini Naidu was known as "the Nightingale of India"; her poetry was considered as beautiful as song. As well as a poet and playwright, she was an activist for Indian independence (her anti-British activities earned her several prison sentences) and was the first woman to be President of the Indian National Congress and Governor of Uttar Pradesh.

She grew up in Hyderabad, and wrote poetry from an early age. Her highly educated parents took the unusual step of sending her to King's College, London, on a scholarship. In London she met the literary critic Edmund Gosse, who encouraged her poetry. Naidu named her first poetry collection *The Golden Threshold* and dedicated it to Gosse, because, she said, he "first showed me the way to the golden threshold".

"Nightfall in the City of Hyderabad" is a poetic tourist guide to her home town; her readers become travellers. "She transports us there through our senses," said Amanda.

Peridote is a yellow-green mineral, also called chrysolite. The Char Minar is the 16th-century mosque which with its four minarets dominates the old town.

Evenen in the Village

BY WILLIAM BARNES 1801–1886

Now the light o' the west is a-turn'd to gloom,
An' the men be at hwome vrom ground;
An' the bells be a-zenden all down the Coombe
From tower, their mwoansome sound.
An' the wind is still,
An' the house-dogs do bark,
An' the rooks be a-vled to the elems high an' dark,
An' the water do roar at mill.

An' the flickeren light drough the window-peane
Vrom the candle's dull fleame do shoot,
An' young Jemmy the smith is a-gone down leane,
A-playen his shrill-vaiced flute.
An' the miller's man
Do zit down at his ease
On the seat that is under the cluster o' trees,
Wi' his pipe an' his cider can.

William Barnes' formal education ended at 13, but he
taught himself Italian, Persian, German, French, Latin

and Greek. He was fascinated by dialect, and often wrote poems – like this one – using the voices of his native Dorset. He played the violin, piano and flute. Several members of the group commented on the musicality of "Evenen in the Village". "It's nearly all sounds," said Shelagh, "the bells, the dogs, the water, the rooks, the flute..." "And yet somehow it's very visual too, with the dark elms and the candle at the window," said Henrietta. Mike F liked the miller's man sitting with his pipe and his cider at the end of a day's work; no judgement is passed, no moral is drawn.

Barnes ran a school in Dorchester; the young Thomas Hardy worked for the firm of architects next door. If Hardy found himself in a dispute about a linguistic point with any of his colleagues, he would run round to Barnes, who would settle it. Cresta recalled Hardy's poem "Afterwards", in which he hopes to be remembered after death as someone with acute powers of observation – "will the neighbours say,/'He was a man who used to notice such things'?" – and remarked that William Barnes must have been exactly that kind of man.

11

HEARTH & HOME

Hearth and home – two of the most evocative words in the language. Identity, security, permanence – all are closely connected to the idea of home.

Verses upon the Burning of our House, July 10th, 1666

BY ANNE BRADSTREET 1612–1672

Here Follows Some Verses Upon the Burning of Our house, July 10th. 1666. Copied Out of a Loose Paper.

In silent night when rest I took,
For sorrow neer I did not look,
I waken'd was with thundring nois
And Piteous shreiks of dreadfull voice.
That fearfull sound of fire and fire,
Let no man know is my Desire.

I, starting up, the light did spye,
And to my God my heart did crye
To strengthen me in my Distresse
And not to leave me succourlesse.
Then coming out behold a space,
The flame consume my dwelling place.

And, when I could no longer look,
I blest his Name that gave and took,
That layd my goods now in the dust:
Yea so it was, and so 'twas just.
It was his own, it was not mine;
Far be it that I should repine.

He might of All justly bereft
But yet sufficient for us left.
When by the Ruines oft I past,
My sorrowing eyes aside did cast,
And here and there the places spye
Where oft I sate, and long did lye.

Here stood that Trunk, and there that chest;
There lay that store I counted best:
My pleasant things in ashes lye,
And them behold no more shall I.
Under thy roof no guest shall sitt,
Nor at thy Table eat a bitt.

No pleasant tale shall 'ere be told
Nor things recounted done of old.
No Candle 'ere shall shine in Thee,
Nor bridegroom's voice 'ere heard shall bee.
In silence ever shalt thou lye,
Adieu, Adieu; All's vanity.

Then streight I 'gin my heart to chide,
And did thy wealth on earth abide?
Didst fix thy hope on mouldring dust,
The arm of flesh didst make thy trust?
Raise up thy thoughts above the skye
That dunghill mists away may flie.

Thou hast a house on high erect,
Framed by that mighty Architect,
With glory richly furnished,
Stands permanent though this bee fled.
It's purchased, and paid for too
By Him who hath enough to doe.

A Prise so vast as is unknown,
Yet, by his Gift is made thine own.
Ther's wealth enough, I need no more;
Farewell, my Pelf, farewell, my Store.
The world no longer let me Love,
My hope and Treasure lyes Above.

Anne Bradstreet was the first Puritan writer in American literature, and the first female to be published in both the Old and the New World; her debut collection, *The Tenth Muse Lately Sprung Up in America*, received considerable attention when it was published in 1650. With her family, she migrated from England to America after the founding of the Massachusetts Bay Colony in 1630. She was educated and cultured; both her father and her husband became Governors of the Colony, and both were involved in the founding of Harvard.

The family – she had eight children – were living comfortably and respectably in North Andover when a fire destroyed their house on the night of 10 July 1666 (coincidentally, the year of the Great Fire of London). Sue said, "What's touching is that she's trying not to mind, but yet showing us that she does mind, dreadfully." Sarah N found the line "Nor bridegroom's voice 'ere heard shall bee" particularly poignant; "She's been looking forward to having her daughters' weddings there, and now it can't ever happen." We agreed it was a very female poem. Her pride and joy had been the comfort and hospitality of her house, and she would need all her faith to adjust to its loss. We were touched, too, by her empathetic worry about how busy God must be: "Him who hath enough to doe".

Her enormous collection of books was reduced to ash, like almost everything else.

Stuff

BY ELAINE FEINSTEIN 1930–2019

Here we came in hot July, with the treasures
of a whole life together shambled in boxes
to be unwrapped and set out in new places:
the ebon carving of Rama's wife, Sita,
each hair precisely cut, the puppets
from Prague, heavy art deco goblets,
a Sung fan discovered in South East Asia,
a cherry-wood flute player. You were

always eager to explore, and equally pleased
to investigate auction rooms or an Oxfam shop.
In a hardware store, you discovered elegance in
a simple tool for shaving slivers of cheese.
Even caches of paper clips and staplers
hold your presence, and the screws,
the Araldite stored under the stairs

you often used to mend the backs of chairs.
Not to speak of the iMac, in which your spirit
still continues: nets of thoughts intensely lived.

And most of all, in walnut drawers beneath
the table by our bed where once you kept
sleeping pills and indigestion tablets:
your hearing aid, your spectacles, your teeth.

This poem was suggested by Amanda. After Amanda's husband died, a friend gave her *Talking to the Dead*, Elaine Feinstein's collection of poems about the loss of her husband. At first, Amanda couldn't bear to read it, but when she did, she found poignant parallels with her own experience. "We had moved house and we were still unpacking boxes when Christopher died six months later. I love the way 'Stuff' mixes the mundane and the exotic (aren't most houses like that after a time?) and how, in the end, those items which have a value above rubies are the most everyday: spectacles, pills, false teeth. But at the moment of death they revert to being everyday things again, now without a purpose; just detritus left behind by the receding tide of life."

Many of us have had the experience of going through "stuff" after a death, and feeling paralysed by indecision about what to do with objects, some of them ugly or useless or both, which still seem to hold the presence of the person who's gone. Elaine Feinstein's tone is matter-of-fact. Her sentences, rearranged, would be almost indistinguishable from prose. But through this carefully considered ordinariness she allows the "stuff" to reveal a man, a marriage, a life. "By putting his teeth at the end like that, it makes you feel so sad for her," said Kirsty.

Gratitude

ADDRESSED TO LADY HESKETH

BY WILLIAM COWPER 1731–1800

This cap, that so stately appears,
With ribbon-bound tassel on high,
Which seems by the crest that it rears
Ambitious of brushing the sky:
This cap to my cousin I owe;
She gave it, and gave me beside,
Wreathed into an elegant bow,
The ribbon with which it is tied.

This wheel-footed studying chair,
Contriv'd both for toil and repose,
Wide-elbow'd, and wadded with hair,
In which I both scribble and doze,
Bright-studded to dazzle the eyes,
And rival in lustre of that
In which, or Astronomy lies,
Fair Cassiopeia sat:

These carpets, so soft to the foot,
Caledonia's traffic and pride!
Oh spare them, ye knights of the boot,
Escaped from a cross-country ride!
This table and mirror within,

Secure from collision and dust,
At which I oft shave cheek and chin,
And periwig nicely adjust:

This moveable structure of shelves,
For its beauty admired and its use,
And charg'd with octavos and twelves,
The gayest I had to produce;
Where, flaming in scarlet and gold,
My poems enchanted I view,
And hope, in due time, to behold
My Iliad and Odyssey too:

This china, that decks the alcove,
Which here people call a boufet,
But what the gods call it above
Has ne'er been reveal'd to us yet:
These curtains, that keep the room warm,
Or cool, as the season demands,
Those stoves, that for pattern and form,
Seem the labour of Mulciber's hands.

All these are not half that I owe
To one, from our earliest youth
To me ever ready to show
Benignity, friendship, and truth;
For Time, the destroyer, declar'd,
And foe of our perishing kind,

If even her face he has spar'd,
Much less could he alter her mind.

Thus compass'd about with the goods
And chattels of leisure and ease,
I indulge my poetical moods
In many such fancies as these;
And fancies I fear they will seem –
Poets' goods are not often so fine;
The poets will swear that I dream,
When I sing of the splendour of mine.

Cowper was a sensitive plant – indeed, he wrote a poem comparing an oyster and a sensitive plant to a poet. Traumatised by the early death of his mother, bullied at school, strongly afflicted by melancholia and fears of eternal damnation, he depended throughout his life on the kindness of friends and relations. In "Gratitude" he praises his cousin Lady Hesketh, who has provided him with so many objects designed to give him the perfect environment in which to write his poetry. Perhaps no other English poet before Betjeman drew so much of his inspiration from fixtures and fittings; Cowper really relished domesticity. "These are the things that make him feel safe," said Pepe.

In the fourth verse, he tells of his delight at contemplating his books – "octavos and twelves" are book sizes – including his own poems, resplendent on the bookshelves his cousin has given him. Soon, he hopes they will be joined by the translations of Homer he's working on – "*my* Iliad and Odyssey". In a local second-hand bookshop I self-indulgently bought a handsome two-volume edition of Cowper because it was "flaming in scarlet and gold" like the edition he mentions here.

Cowper was one of Jane Austen's favourite poets.

Cuckoo Spit

BY DOROTHY NIMMO 1932–2001

Now spring is sprung the leaping sap
gorges the ride with bitter green,
the undergrowth is clutching at the knees,
something is going cuckoo in the trees.

Sluggish and summery the river flows
along the verge the nettles growing rank,
something is going cuckoo on the bank.

Over the fields the seasons hustle past
the eggs are hatched the young ones cry for food,
something is going cuckoo in the wood.

Against her ears her dish-cloth hands are pressed.
Someone is going cuckoo in the nest.

A *cri de coeur* from a woman stifled and stymied by motherhood and domesticity. The delights of the season are
all inverted; growth is "bitter" and "rank", and the plants
clutch at the knees like tyrannical toddlers. Shelagh
noticed how punctuation is all but abandoned in the

third section, to mimic the rush of deluging demands, and is reinstated in the closing couplet; the two full stops like bolts to imitate entrapment.

Dorothy Nimmo, mother of four, "ran away from home" in middle age to join a Quaker community.

The South Country

BY HILAIRE BELLOC 1870–1953

When I am living in the Midlands
That are sodden and unkind,
I light my lamp in the evening:
My work is left behind;
And the great hills of the South Country
Come back into my mind.

The great hills of the South Country
They stand along the sea;
And it's there walking in the high woods
That I could wish to be,
And the men that were boys when I was a boy
Walking along with me.

The men that live in North England
I saw them for a day:
Their hearts are set upon the waste fells,
Their skies are fast and grey;
From their castle-walls a man may see
The mountains far away.

The men that live in West England
They see the Severn strong,
A-rolling on rough water brown

Light aspen leaves along.
They have the secret of the Rocks,
And the oldest kind of song.

But the men that live in the South Country
Are the kindest and most wise,
They get their laughter from the loud surf,
And the faith in their happy eyes
Comes surely from our Sister the Spring
When over the sea she flies;
The violets suddenly bloom at her feet,
She blesses us with surprise.

I never get between the pines
But I smell the Sussex air;
Nor I never come on a belt of sand
But my home is there,
And along the sky the line of the Downs
So noble and so bare.

A lost thing could I never find,
Nor a broken thing mend:
And I fear I shall be all alone
When I get towards the end.
Who will there be to comfort me
Or who will be my friend?

I will gather and carefully make my friends
Of the men of the Sussex Weald;
They watch the stars from silent folds,
They stiffly plough the field.
By them and the God of the South Country
My poor soul shall be healed.

If I ever become a rich man,
Or if ever I grow to be old,
I will build a house with deep thatch
To shelter me from the cold,
And there shall the Sussex songs be sung
And the story of Sussex told.

I will hold my house in the high wood
Within a walk of the sea,
And the men that were boys when I was a boy
Shall sit and drink with me.

"I've got this one pinned to my kitchen wall!" exclaimed
Sue, and we Sussex-dwellers all indulged in a moment
of local pride. Everyone privately knows that the place
they call home is the best place in the world, so it's nice
to find a poem that puts the feeling into words. And the

fact that Belloc uses my absolutely favourite word of all – Weald – sets the seal on it.

Enemies of Belloc (he had many, and it doesn't do to look too closely into his political opinions) might call this poem superficial, meretricious, sentimental. I think the seventh verse redeems it. "A lost thing could I never find,/Nor a broken thing mend" – there's real pathos, and real self-knowledge, in those lines. The "thing" could be a watch, a bicycle, a plate, a heart. Belloc was a big blundering bear of a man who rode roughshod through life, but he cared passionately about many things, and one of them was Sussex. He more or less achieved his vision of the last two verses; he lived at King's Land, Shipley – not thatched, but an old Sussex house, with a windmill next door. Here he lived by candlelight, mainly on bread, cheese and beer. In his old age his friends did indeed gather round and tell the story of Sussex – or at least, they listened to Belloc telling it. He died, aged nearly 83, after falling into the fire in his study.

The House was Quiet and the World was Calm

BY WALLACE STEVENS 1882–1955

The house was quiet and the world was calm.
The reader became the book; and summer night

Was like the conscious being of the book.
The house was quiet and the world was calm.

The words were spoken as if there was no book,
Except that the reader leaned above the page,

Wanted to lean, wanted much most to be
The scholar to whom his book is true, to whom

The summer night is like a perfection of thought.
The house was quiet because it had to be.

The quiet was part of the meaning, part of the mind:
The access of perfection to the page.

And the world was calm. The truth in a calm world,
In which there is no other meaning, itself

Is calm, itself is summer and night, itself
Is the reader leaning late and reading there.

In this, one of his more accessible poems, Wallace Stevens merges act and process, external and internal, visible and invisible. There are several "ing" endings – being, meaning, leaning, reading – to draw us into the experience that leads to the crystallisation of "truth". He uses many variants of "being" and "becoming", as the house, world, reader, book, summer and night draw together in transcendent harmony.

"The title is an absolute ideal state for me," said Clare.

The Old Love

BY KATHARINE TYNAN 1859–1931

Out of my door I step into
The country, all her scent and dew,
Nor travel there by a hard road,
Dusty and far from my abode.

The country washes to my door
Green miles on miles in soft uproar,
The thunder of the woods, and then
The backwash of green surf again.

Beyond the feverfew and stocks,
The guelder-rose and hollyhocks;
Outside my trellised porch a tree
Of lilac frames a sky for me.

A stretch of primrose and pale green
To hold the tender Hesper in;
Hesper that by the moon makes pale
Her silver keel and silver sail.

The country silence wraps me quite,
Silence and song and pure delight;
The country beckons all the day
Smiling, and but a step away.

This is that country seen across
How many a league of love and loss,
Prayed for and longed for; and as far
As fountains in the desert are.

This is that country at my door,
Whose fragrant airs run on before,
And call me when the first birds stir
In the green wood to walk with her.

Katharine Tynan grew up on a small farm in County
Dublin. She came to know both Gerard Manley Hopkins and W.B. Yeats well, and hints of their influence can
be felt in this tender evocation of a beloved place. "I love
the 'green miles on miles in soft uproar'", said Henrietta.
"It feels very Irish."

The Shortest and the Sweetest of Songs

BY GEORGE MACDONALD 1824–1905

Come
Home.

Who said Victorians were verbose? George MacDonald, perhaps best known today as the author of *The Princess and the Goblin*, has put together two common words in a way that makes them pulse with the very essence of poetry. By placing one under the other he showcases both. "Come" is both a command and a plea, full of yearning; "Home" stands for warmth, safety, completion, everything a heart desires. They look as if they rhyme, but they don't, which leaves the poem unresolved; the long vowel sound in "Home" stretches out far beyond the confines of the tiny "song". We know that this is not, say, the peremptory bark of a parent summoning a wayward child; we feel, without being told, that this is a passionate plea from someone who fears they are losing the love of their life. "How clever!" exclaimed Caroline T.

12

LOSS, AGE & DEATH

Poetry is a way of outwitting death. Several of the poems in this section are autobiographical; through them, the author lives on in the mind of the reader. We share Owen's dread, Jonson's loss, Donne's resolute joy, and in the process we investigate our own mortality, and learn to accept that we will one day "sleep in the ground" like the ancient Irish kings.

Call for the Robin Redbreast

BY JOHN WEBSTER C.1580– C.1632

Call for the Robin-Red-brest and the wren,
Since ore shadie groves they hover,
And with leaves and flowres do cover
The friendlesse bodies of unburied men.
Call unto his funerall Dole
The Ante, the field-mouse, and the mole
To rear him hillockes, that shall keepe him warme,
And (when gay tombes are robb'd) sustaine no harme,
But keepe the wolfe far hence, that's foe to men,
For with his nailes hee'l dig them up agen.

This chilling dirge comes from Act 5 Scene V of *The White Devil*, a Jacobean drama of murder, deception, corruption and madness. Appearances are never what they seem and evil is covered – unsuccessfully – with a gloss of virtue. "I can't get rid of those last two lines – they really stick," said Olivia.

The dirge is sung by Cornelia, who has gone mad as a result of the murder of her son Marcello by her other son, Flamineo; she is "grown a very old woman in two hours". In her madness, Cornelia combines elements of both Ophelia and Lady Macbeth; John Webster was Shakespeare's younger contemporary. "This rosemary is wither'd, pray get fresh;/I would have these herbs grow up in his grave/When I am dead and rotten," she tells the servants as they wrap her son in his winding sheet; "I'll tie a garland here about his head:/'Twill keep my boy from lightning."

His mother's distress (almost) softens the black heart of Flamineo: "I have a strange thing in me, to the which/I cannot give a name, without [unless] it be/ Compassion."

The Unreturning

BY WILFRED OWEN 1893–1918

Suddenly night crushed out the day and hurled
Her remnants over cloud-peaks, thunder-walled.
Then fell a stillness such as harks appalled
When far-gone dead return upon the world.

There watched I for the dead; but no ghost woke.
Each one whom Life exiled I named and called.
But they were all too far, or dumbed, or thralled;
And never one fared back to me or spoke.

Then peered the indefinite unshapen dawn
With vacant gloaming, sad as half-lit minds,
The weak-limned hour when sick men's sighs are drained.
And while I wondered on their being withdrawn,
Gagged by the smothering wing which none unbinds,
I dreaded even a heaven with doors so chained.

Owen wrote a first version of this in 1912 or 1913 as an
exploration of religious doubt, then revised it in 1918
when his war experience had made him all too familiar
with "the unreturning".

Amanda suggested this poem. "It's apocalyptic," said Clare. "That opening is like lobbing a hand grenade," said Sue.

The Nightjar

BY HENRY NEWBOLT 1862–1938

We loved our Nightjar, but she would not stay with us.
We had found her lying as dead, but soft and warm,
Under the apple tree beside the old thatched wall.
Two days we kept her in a basket by the fire,
Fed her, and thought she might well live – till suddenly
In the very moment of most confiding hope
She raised herself all tense, quivered and drooped and
    died.
Tears sprang into my eyes – why not? the heart of man

Soon sets itself to love a living companion,
The more so if by chance it asks some care of him.
And this one had the kind of loveliness that goes
Far deeper than the optic nerve – full fathom five
To the soul's ocean cave, where Wonder and Reason
Tell their alternate dreams of how the world was made.
So wonderful she was – her wings the wings of night
But powdered here and there with tiny golden clouds

And wave-lined markings like sea ripples on the sand.
O how I wish I might never forget that bird –,
Never!
        But even now, like all beauty of earth,
She is fading from me into the dusk of Time.

The sensitivity of this poem surprised us, coming as it does from the pen of a poet usually summed up, slightly sarcastically, with the single word "stirring". Sir Henry Newbolt wrote the much anthologised and much parodied "Vitai Lampada" ("There's a breathless hush in the Close tonight... 'Play up! play up! and play the game!'") and "Drake's Drum" ("Capten, art tha sleepin' there below?"). He also had a huge influence on how English was taught in schools at home and throughout the Empire. As adviser to Lloyd George's government, his 1921 paper, known as "The Newbolt Report", established a literary canon as well as providing a framework for the "correct" teaching of English language. So, directly or indirectly, he's had an effect on most of us.

"The Nightjar" feels like a private, contemplative poem. "They're quite ugly birds at first sight," said Mike F, "but he makes you see the beauty when you look close up." The bird's death touches Newbolt's heart, its beauty feeds his imagination, the mystery of its creation reaches into his soul; the whole experience enlarges his humanity.

We talked about our own attempts to save the lives of wild birds, and of our feelings of guilt and responsibility when these attempts failed, as they almost inevitably do. Only Michael W could boast of success, in the form of a jackdaw who lived and throve for several years.

The Old Familiar Faces

BY CHARLES LAMB 1775–1834

I have had playmates, I have had companions,
In my days of childhood, in my joyful schooldays,
All, all are gone, the old familiar faces.

I have been laughing, I have been carousing,
Drinking late, sitting late, with my bosom cronies,
All, all are gone, the old familiar faces.

I loved a love once, fairest among women;
Closed are her doors on me, I must not see her –
All, all are gone, the old familiar faces.

I have a friend, a kinder friend has no man;
Like an ingrate, I left my friend abruptly;
Left him, to muse on the old familiar faces.

Ghost-like, I paced round the haunts of my childhood.
Earth seemed a desert I was bound to traverse,
Seeking to find the old familiar faces.

Friend of my bosom, thou more than a brother,
Why wert not thou born in my father's dwelling?
So might we talk of the old familiar faces –

How some they have died, and some they have left me,
And some are taken from me; all are departed;
All, all are gone, the old familiar faces.

The critic E.V. Lucas called Charles Lamb "the most loveable figure in English literature". He certainly needed the love of his many friends to help him through life. His older sister Mary, also a writer, suffered from periods of insanity – as did Lamb himself. On 22 September 1796 Mary, preparing dinner, shoved the apprentice girl living with the family out of her way. Mrs Lamb yelled at her; Mary lunged, and stabbed her mother through the heart. Charles leapt forward and wrested the knife from Mary's hand; their father was wounded in the scuffle.

Charles devoted himself to Mary's case, installing her in a private madhouse in Islington. On trial for the murder of her mother, Mary escaped hanging when the jury returned a verdict of "lunacy". After their father's death three years later, Charles took Mary out of the asylum and set up home with her, an arrangement that lasted until the end of his life. In her good periods, they collaborated on their *Tales from Shakespeare*, written for children. Their informal literary salon attracted friends such as Wordsworth, Coleridge, Shelley, Hazlitt, Leigh Hunt.

The "friend of my bosom" is probably Coleridge.

Lamb was small, had a stutter, and had to work as a clerk at the East India Company all his life to pay for his own and Mary's upkeep. His loyalty to her never wavered. Everyone in the group responded sympathetically to the gentle, melancholic speaking voice of "The Old Familiar Faces"; the absence of rhyme, as David pointed out, causes each line to fade sadly away. The poem originally opened with:

Where are they gone, the old familiar faces?
I had a Mother, but she died, and left me,
Died prematurely on a day of horrors –
All, all are gone, the old familiar faces.

These lines were omitted from the 1818 volume of Lamb's collected work.

Winter Nightfall

BY J.C. SQUIRE 1884–1958

The old yellow stucco
Of the time of the Regent
Is flaking and peeling:
The rows of square windows
In the straight yellow building
Are empty and still;
And the dusty dark evergreens
Guarding the wicket
Are draped with wet cobwebs,
And above this poor wilderness
Toneless and sombre
Is the flat of the hill.

They said that a colonel
Who long ago died here
Was the last one to live here:
An old retired colonel,
Some Fraser or Murray,
I don't know his name;
Death came here and summoned him,
And the shells of him vanished
Beyond all speculation;
And silence resumed here,
Silence and emptiness,
And nobody came.

Was it wet when he lived here,
Were the skies dun and hurrying,
Was the rain so irresolute?
Did he watch the night coming,
Did he shiver at nightfall
Before he was dead?
Did the wind go so creepily,
Chilly and puffing,
With drops of cold rain in it?
Was the hill's lifted shoulder
So lowering and menacing,
So dark and so dread?

Did he turn through his doorway
And go to his study,
And light many candles?
And fold in the shutters,
And heap up the fireplace
To fight off the damps?
And muse on his boyhood,
And wonder if India
Ever was real?
And shut out the loneliness
With pig-sticking memoirs
And collections of stamps?

Perhaps. But he's gone now,
He and his furniture
Dispersed now for ever;
And the last of his trophies,
Antlers and photographs,
Heaven knows where.
And there's grass in his gateway,
Grass on his footpath,
Grass on his doorstep;
The garden's grown over,
The well-chain is broken,
The windows are bare.

And I leave him behind me,
For the straggling, discoloured
Rags of the daylight,
And hills and stone walls
And a rick long forgotten
Of blackening hay:
The road pale and sticky,
And cart-ruts and nail marks,
And wind-ruffled puddles,
And the slop of my footsteps
In this desolate country's
Cadaverous clay.

Sir John Collings Squire was an important influence in the British literary world between the wars. Editor of the *London Mercury*, champion of the Georgian poets, and a well-known parodist and anthologist, he was loathed by modernists. Virginia Woolf found him "more repulsive than words can express, and malignant into the bargain". However, his grandson Roger Squire, who kindly gave me permission to use this poem, points out that this was not the whole story: "My grandfather and Virginia Woolf were both members of the Fabian Society and she dined at his house in Chiswick on a number of occasions and he visited her cottage in Rodmell, Sussex, at least once for a weekend. Woolf praised his parodies, and he published a couple of her short stories. There was some mutual admiration, despite the fact that their literary styles were very different."

We were all impressed by "Winter Nightfall". The narrator's natural speaking voice – he's chiefly talking to himself – is shaped lightly into poetry by the dogged rhythm and that single rhyme-pair in each stanza. "That 'Perhaps' is so clever!" said Michael W. The colonel, embodiment of a disappearing world, is imagined with sympathy and deft economy: "And wonder if India / Ever was real" compresses a lifetime. Though the speaker says, "I leave him behind me", he knows that he will face the same fate, as will we all; no one can escape their "winter nightfall". The forsaken garden, the broken well-chain, the blackening hay – sources of renewal – are stopped, and we plod on, aware that we, like the colonel, are no more than "cadaverous clay".

"Winter Nightfall" was first published in 1919. The dreariness and decay suggests an England exhausted by war and uncertain of its future, and, as Roger Squire says, the "cadaverous clay" feels like "a reference to Flanders' fields and trench warfare". The war is over, but its effects permeate everything.

On my First Son

BY BEN JONSON 1572–1637

Farewell, thou child of my right hand, and joy;
My sin was too much hope of thee, lov'd boy.
Seven years thou wert lent to me, and I thee pay,
Exacted by thy fate, on the just day.
O, could I lose all father now! For why
Will man lament the state he should envy?
To have so soon 'scap'd world's and flesh's rage,
And if no other misery, yet age?
Rest in soft peace, and, ask'd, say, "Here doth lie
Ben Jonson his best piece of poetry."
For whose sake henceforth all his vows be such,
As what he loves, may never like too much.

Ben Jonson's seven-year-old son, also named Ben, died
of the plague in 1603. Ben senior was 31, already a successful, if controversial, poet, playwright and actor. His
characteristic self-confidence and energy are evident
even in this intense expression of grief. The bitter tone
of the first eight lines, where Jonson struggles to find rea-
sons to accept his loss, suddenly give way to "rest in soft

peace", which feels all the more tender in contrast with the grappling vigour of what has gone before.

Describing your dead child as your "best piece of poetry" could, I suppose, be seen as arrogant. For me, it feels intensely personal, one of the most moving lines in literature. When I read this aloud, there was a silence. There seemed no right way to discuss a poem about a loss so deeply felt. "I just can't talk about it," said Polly, speaking for everyone.

Jewels in my Hand

BY SASHA MOORSOM 1931–1993

I hold dead friends like jewels in my hand
Watching their brilliance gleam against my palm
Turquoise and emerald, jade, a golden band

All ravages of time they can withstand
Like talismans their grace keeps me from harm
I hold dead friends like jewels in my hand

I see them standing in some borderland
Their heads half-turned, waiting for my arm
Turquoise and emerald, jade, a golden band

I'm not afraid they will misunderstand
My turning to them like a magic charm
I hold dead friends like jewels in my hand
Turquoise and emerald, jade, a golden band

Sasha Moorsom, an artist as well as a poet, died of cancer. Her daughter, who nursed her, wrote: "She refused to let the pain and weakness of her body prevent her from writing poetry and she was still able to see the beauty in everything."

"The repeated rhymes make the poem turn round and round, like a bangle on your arm," said Judith.

Shelagh said "the words feel so spacious – words like grace and charm and time. And the lack of punctuation gives you a sense of eternity."

"Like the jewels, it's brilliant," said Pepe.

Hymne to God my God, in my Sicknesse

BY JOHN DONNE 1572–1631

Since I am comming to that Holy roome,
  Where, with thy Quire of Saints for evermore,
I shall be made thy Musique; As I come
  I tune the Instrument here at the dore,
  And what I must doe then, thinke here before.

Whilst my Physitians by their love are growne
  Cosmographers, and I their Mapp, who lie
Flat on this bed, that by them may be showne
  That this is my South-west discoverie
  Per fretum febris, by these streights to die,

I joy, that in these straits, I see my West;
  For, though theire currants yeeld returne to none,
What shall my West hurt me? As West and East
  In all flatt Maps (and I am one) are one,
  So death doth touch the Resurrection.

Is the Pacifique Sea my home? Or are
  The Easterne riches? Is *Jerusalem*?
Anyan, and *Magellan*, and *Gibraltare*,
  All streights, and none but streights, are wayes to them,
  Whether where *Japhet* dwelt, or *Cham*, or *Sem*.

We thinke that *Paradise* and *Calvarie*,
　　Christs Crosse, and *Adams tree*, stood in one place;
Looke, Lord, and finde both *Adams* met in me;
　　As the first *Adams* sweat surrounds my face,
　　May the last *Adams* blood my soule embrace.

So, in his purple wrapp'd receive mee Lord,
　　By these his thornes give me his other Crowne;
And as to others soules I preach'd thy word,
　　Be this my Text, my Sermon to mine owne,
　　Therfore that he may raise the Lord throws down.

[Japhet, Cham and Sem we're the sons of Noah, who
went off to colonise Europe, Africa and Asia respec-
tively. So by naming them here, Donne means "the
whole world".]

Donne either wrote this during a life-threatening fever-
ous illness in 1623, or else in 1630 when he really was
approaching the end of his life. Dean of St Paul's since
1621, he was no longer the teasing, tricksy, much-
imitated young poet of risqué love lyrics, but instead
had a large following of serious-minded admirers who

packed the cathedral to hear his sermons. But whether trying to persuade women to go to bed with him or his flock to turn to Christ, it remained Donne's poetic habit to put himself at the centre of his argument. The "Hymn to God my God" is both a public and a private poem, his sermon to himself. It is a magnificent attempt to summarise the state of his body, mind and soul, as he approaches the "Holy roome" that waits beyond death. "He's very confident that he'll go there, and not to the other place," said Pam.

Donne lived in an age of exploration, and was enthralled by the rapidly expanding knowledge of the world. In one of the poems of his youth, "Elegie: To His Mistris Going to Bed", he famously addresses his beloved as "O my America! my new found land"; here, his own body becomes a map of the world. The doctors pore over his symptoms, as proud as explorers when they identify which will be the cause of death – "per fretum febris" means "by the strait of fever". Donne turns disaster into triumph – yes, there's no turning back, but as on a map, west must touch east, so his death will result in his resurrection in the next world. Nothing worthwhile or precious can be attained without difficulty. Donne, like Adam, like all humans, must suffer, but through suffering he will reach "the last Adam"– Jesus Christ.

"The way he's put 'I joy' at the beginning of the verse like that," said Clare, "that's wonderful."

The Fort of Rathangan

ANON. 11TH CENTURY IRISH

TRANSLATED BY KUNO MEYER 1911

The fort over against the oak-wood,
Once it was Bruidge's, it was Cathal's,
It was Aed's, it was Ailill's,
It was Conaing's, it was Cuiline's,
And it was Maelduin's;
The fort remains after each in his turn –
And the kings asleep in the ground.

Kuno Meyer was German, but became a great Celtic scholar, and founded the School of Irish Learning in Dublin. The Irish were grateful to him for revealing their ancient literary past to them, and I am grateful to him for providing this little poem which, with its solid combination of finality and continuity, and its incantatory naming of the local kings, feels like an appropriate note on which to end this book.

Acknowledgements

I'd like to thank the Short Books team for all their efforts on behalf of this book – Aurea Carpenter, Rebecca Nicolson, Evie Dunne, Helena Sutcliffe, Paul Bougourd, Catherine Gibbs and Katherine Stroud.

Many thanks to Amanda Helm for her invaluable help and advice, and to Annalise Orban for her beautiful illustrations (annalise.orban@gmail.com).

I'm very grateful to the many friends who have introduced me to various poems, and to all members of the Tuesday gatherings for their enthusiasm, support and friendship.

Permissions

The author and publishers gratefully acknowledge permission to reprint copyright material in this book as follows:

W.H. AUDEN: "Roman Wall Blues". Copyright © W.H. Auden. Reprinted by permission of Curtis Brown Ltd.

HILAIRE BELLOC: "The South Country". Copyright © Hilaire Belloc. Reprinted by permission of Pollinger Ltd/ Peters Fraser and Dunlop.

JOHN BETJEMAN: "Indoor Games at Newbury" from *Collected Poems* by John Betjeman. Copyright © John Betjeman. Reprinted by permission of John Murray, an imprint of Hodder and Stoughton Ltd.

EDMUND BLUNDEN: "Pillbox" from *Undertones of War* by Edmund Blunden. Copyright © Edmund Blunden. Reprinted by permission of David Higham Associates on behalf of The Edmund Blunden Literary Estate.

CHARLES CAUSLEY: "Eden Rock" from *Collected Poems* by Charles Causley. Copyright © Charles Causley. Reprinted by permission of David Higham Associates.

ELIZABETH COATSWORTH: "On a Night of Snow". Copyright © Elizabeth Coatsworth. Reprinted by permission of The Marsh Agency Ltd on behalf of the Estate of Elizabeth Coatsworth.

Index of Authors